Praise for *Surrender Your Story*

"This book feels like you are at a coffee conversation with Tara—as she tells you her own story of surrendering control of her life to the Lord and what she has learned along the way. For anyone in a season wrestling with giving God complete control over every single plan in their life, I could not think of a better read and better reminder that He writes the best stories."

—Sadie Robertson Huff, *New York Times* bestselling author, speaker, and founder of Live Original

"Tara Sun is a fresh, deeply wise voice worth listening to because she faithfully listens to the Word Himself. With keen, biblically rooted insights that keep you turning the pages, Tara writes for every tender heart that deeply longs for an authentic story of wholeness."

—Ann Voskamp, *New York Times* bestselling author of *One Thousand Gifts*

"To the planners, Type As, and borderline control freaks . . . this one's for us. With beautiful transparency and truth straight from Scripture, Tara reminds us how surrendering your story is truly God's call to simplicity. Don't just read this book, put it into practice!"

—Michelle Myers, cofounder of She Works His Way and author of the Conversational Commentary series

"If you care deeply about your relationship with the Lord but also sometimes struggle with trusting Him with your life's plans, then this book will be your guide. Through her own honest journey and deep biblical insights, Tara helps us discover the true beauty of surrender."

—Ashley Morgan Jackson, staff and content writer at Proverbs 31 Ministries and author

"Trusting God with our story is such a hard thing to do. I'm so glad to have Tara's inspiring and encouraging voice to walk us through it!"

—Stephanie May Wilson, author and host of *The Girls Night* podcast

"Tara is fun, real, and raw. I am in many ways a type A control freak, and this book made me feel seen. If you struggle to find peace in the chaos and feel anxious when things don't go as planned, this book is for you. Our culture needs to learn the art of surrender on a more radical level. This book deeply spoke to and challenged me in ways I didn't even know I needed."

—Kait Tomlin, bestselling author, dating coach,
and founder of Heart of Dating

"*Surrender Your Story* is a loud and loving call to the body of Christ for such a time as this. As we navigate living in a culture that prides itself on self-sufficiency and independence, Tara urges us to get off the throne of our own lives and allow God to take His rightful place as the Lord of our lives. This message invites us into a deeper walk of faith with an overarching anthem that sings 'God I trust you and where you go, I'll go.'"

—Mariela Rosario, author and founder of She Speaks Fire

"In her book, *Surrender Your Story*, Tara Sun invites us to embrace the freedom found in ditching the concept of control. In a world saturated in messages that tell us to 'Take control of our lives,' Tara offers heartfelt stories and pours out solid biblical teachings that point her reader to this soul-anchoring truth: there's freedom found in surrendering our lives to Christ. This book is timely and shelf-worthy! A must read for women of all ages."

—Cassandra Speer, bestselling author, Bible teacher,
and vice president of Her True Worth

"In a world obsessed with control the truth remains: our lives are in the hands of a good and sovereign God who is present, active, and working through it all. In her new book, *Surrender Your Story*, Tara Sun invites us into her story and lovingly leads us. Like sitting down with a close friend over coffee, she gives us the courage to discover the freedom God offers when we yield our way to His."

—Ruth Schwenk, coauthor of *Trusting God in All the Things*

"With boldness and clarity, Tara Sun offers a fresh, new voice on a problem that has plagued humanity since the beginning: control. In *Surrender Your Story* Tara dismantles the lies we tell ourselves about self-sufficiency and then guides us to trusting God, the only one who holds the plan for our lives. I know this book will speak powerfully to the hearts of women who want to surrender their stories to Him, once and for all."

—Jennifer Dukes Lee, author of *It's All Under Control* and *Growing Slow*

"To the girl who isn't so sure that trusting God is worth the risk, this book will challenge and encourage you in the truth that God is worthy of our surrender and His ways are better than what we could ever plan on our own. To the girl who is weary from holding onto control with such a tight grip, this book will show you the full rest and freedom that comes when we live fully dependent upon God."

—Emma Mae McDaniel, author, speaker, and host of the *Have You Heard?* podcast

"Tara does a beautiful job of helping us see why the struggle with control can be such a difficult one, but she doesn't stop there. These truth-filled pages are filled with more encouragement than you could possibly imagine. From sharing her own story of learning how to cultivate a heart of surrender, to sharing biblical examples and tangible takeaways for how to live and enjoy your life—hardships included—from a genuine place of surrender before the Lord, this book will not disappoint."

—Elle Cardel, founder of Daughter of Delight

"When reading Tara's book, not only was I cheering for and celebrating my friend's incredible work, but I was also motivated to surrender control to God in areas of my own life where I had not yet given Him 100 percent. With kindness, love, and truth Tara brings forth encouragement and perspective as to why God's best is the best for our lives and how doing life in submission and surrender to Him is beautiful, exciting, and always worth it. I can't wait to see how this book encourages others in their own personal stories of freedom and fullness in all God has for them!"

—Kirby Kelly, speaker and host of the *Bought + Beloved* podcast

Surrender
YOUR Story

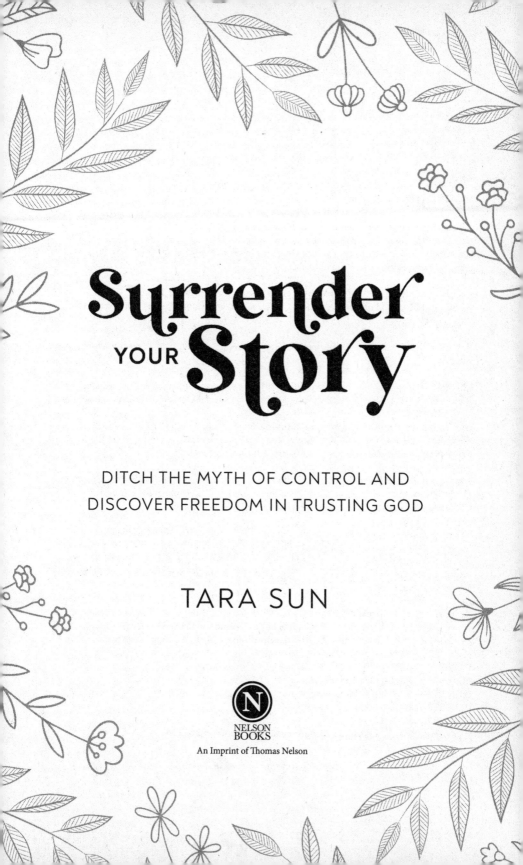

Surrender
YOUR Story

DITCH THE MYTH OF CONTROL AND
DISCOVER FREEDOM IN TRUSTING GOD

TARA SUN

NELSON
BOOKS

An Imprint of Thomas Nelson

Surrender Your Story

© 2023 by Tara Sun Snyder

Published in Nashville, Tennessee, by Nelson Books, an imprint of Thomas Nelson. Nelson Books and Thomas Nelson are registered trademarks of HarperCollins Christian Publishing, Inc.

Published in association with William K. Jensen Literary Agency, 119 Bampton Court, Eugene, Oregon 97404.

Thomas Nelson titles may be purchased in bulk for educational, business, fundraising, or sales promotional use. For information, please email SpecialMarkets@ThomasNelson.com.

Unless otherwise noted, Scripture quotations are taken from the ESV® Bible (The Holy Bible, English Standard Version®). Copyright © 2001 by Crossway, a publishing ministry of Good News Publishers. Used by permission. All rights reserved.

Scripture quotations marked CSB® are taken from the Christian Standard Bible®, Copyright © 2017 by Holman Bible Publishers. Used by permission. Christian Standard Bible® and CSB® are federally registered trademarks of Holman Bible Publishers.

Scripture quotations marked NIV are taken from The Holy Bible, New International Version®, NIV®. Copyright © 1973, 1978, 1984, 2011 by Biblica, Inc.® Used by permission of Zondervan. All rights reserved worldwide. www.Zondervan.com. The "NIV" and "New International Version" are trademarks registered in the United States Patent and Trademark Office by Biblica, Inc.®

Scripture quotations marked NLT are taken from the Holy Bible, New Living Translation, copyright © 1996, 2004, 2015 by Tyndale House Foundation. Used by permission of Tyndale House Publishers, Inc., Carol Stream, Illinois 60188. All rights reserved.

ISBN 978-1-4002-3920-7 (HC)
ISBN 978-1-4002-3922-1 (audiobook)
ISBN 978-1-4002-3921-4 (eBook)
ISBN 978-1-4002-4366-2 (ITPE)

Library of Congress Control Number: 2022043551

Printed in the United States of America
22 23 24 25 26 LBC 5 4 3 2 1

*To my husband, the love of my life, and my son,
the joy of our lives. I am forever thankful that
God, our good and gracious Author, chose to
write our stories together. Love you forever.*

*To my online community and followers but more than
that, my friends. This is for you. Here's to continuing
to know, love, and live God's Word together.*

Contents

CHAPTER 1

The Myth of Control

> Nothing is a surprise to God; nothing is a
> setback to His plans; nothing can thwart His
> purposes; and nothing is beyond His control.
> JONI EARECKSON TADA

IT WAS THE FIRST TIME that I heard the audible voice of God, as clear as day. It was almost as if it were projected over the loud-speakers across campus.

Tara, you are not supposed to be here.

I frantically scanned my biology class, wondering if anyone else had heard that loud voice too. But as I looked around, all I saw were hundreds of eager students, aggressively jotting down notes as the professor explained the exciting careers we could have one day in the medical field.

A few minutes later, the professor shut off the slideshow and dismissed the class. Confused and flustered, I shuffled out of the lecture with my classmates. I walked back to my dorm with what felt like a literal dark cloud hovering over me—like the ones you see in cartoons. I ran upstairs to my room, dropped my backpack, slumped down at my desk, and began to bawl my eyes out.

Through mascara-stained tears, I cried out to God, "What do You mean I'm 'not supposed to be here'? Isn't this the plan? What could You possibly have for me that's better than this?"

A knot grew in my stomach. Ever since I was a little girl, I'd had a mental blueprint for my life. The plan was simple:

I would coast through school with good grades.
I would get accepted into my college of choice and excel in a biology degree.
I would apply for medical school and become a doctor.
Along the way I would meet a nice Christian man, and we would get married and have kids once I was at a solid place in my career.

And up until that morning, everything seemed to be going pretty much according to that plan. My blueprint seemed to be working.

But in that lecture hall, it felt like God had had taken a quick look at my carefully crafted blueprint, crumpled it up, tossed it in the wastebasket, and said *nope* with about twenty exclamation marks. Anger and bitterness began to plant seeds in my heart.

Why would God say no to my plans? *God, aren't You good?*

Don't You love me? Don't You work all things for my good? Why don't You want this to happen?

From where I was standing the blueprint I had mapped out looked solid—no deceptive or sinful motivations, nothing that seemed to dishonor God or deviate from what the Bible said. But now my foundation was starting to slip beneath me. The rock I had built my life on was looking more like sand. The blueprint ink was fading, blurring, clouding—and it terrified me.

Now, friend, you would think that after literally hearing God say, *You're not supposed to be here,* I would listen. But, sadly, I was not ready to let go. I was determined to salvage my plan, because the truth is, I thought I knew better than God. I thought that if I tried a little harder or pivoted just so, God would eventually come around to seeing things my way. He would take back what He said, and I wouldn't have to confront reality.

That evening I nestled into bed earlier than my roommates. Self-pity and I had a sleepover, feeling sorry for ourselves and the fact that God had just dropped a bomb on us. My mind darted from one idea to another, wondering how I could still make my blueprint work. But what happened next is something I will never forget.

From Clenched Fists to Open Hands

The Holy Spirit that I was trying oh-so-hard to quench that day prompted me to look down at my hands. I didn't really feel like listening to His voice, but I reluctantly brought my hands out from under the sheets to look at them. They were balled into tight fists. You know when you clench your hands so hard that they start turning red with pockets of white, with the blood flow restricted by the intensity of your grip? That's exactly what my hands looked like. My eyes instantly welled up with tears.

It was as if God was saying to me, *See your fists? Gripping and holding on so tightly? That, my dear, is what you have been doing with your life. It's time to stop fighting and it's time to surrender to Me.*

But Isn't It Good to Be "In Control"?

You might be wondering why I was so shaken when God told me it was time to rethink my life plan. After all, I understood at some level that it's a good thing to trust and follow God. It's a theme that I had read countless times in Scripture and heard numerous times in church. You'd think I would have handled His wake-up call better!

But here's the thing—I really thought I was already doing everything *right*.

Though I wasn't aware of it at the time, I'd absorbed a lot of messages that complicated and confused my understanding of who is truly in control. Eventually, I came to realize that the control I believed I had over my life was based on a myth—a myth that has seeped into popular thinking nowadays. There are plenty of reasons for this myth's popularity, but I believe a lot of it goes back to the concept of *manifestation*. It's time for a mini history lesson.

The Problem with Manifestation

Helena Blavatsky was one of the most popular (and controversial) "spiritual instructors" of the nineteenth century. Her reputation grew quickly, thanks to her teachings about how humanity was defined and directed by their thought life. In her book *The Secret Doctrine*, she taught people that they had abilities within themselves, their thoughts, and their minds to shape reality and push past any limitation.

Similarly, Thomas Troward was a nineteenth-century psychologist who believed that the human mind was an untapped source of potential, capable of shaping reality. Check out this quote from one of his lectures: "Belief in limitation is the one and only thing that causes limitation."[1]

Then, in 1906, William Walker Atkinson introduced his version of a philosophy called the "law of attraction." The law of attraction stemmed from Hindu religion, which had begun to pique the interest of people in the Western world. To keep it short and sweet, Atkinson believed that people could develop positive magnetism that would attract good things into their lives. By strengthening their willpower and improving their focus, they could bring about not only physical and mental health but also positive outcomes.

There's a common thread that connects these teachings. They all promoted the idea of *manifestation*—the power within an individual's own self to identify, control, and conjure up good things and opportunities. And through Blavatsky, Troward, and Atkinson (along with a host of similar writers and teachers), manifestation worked its way eventually into mainstream thinking.

The idea sounds pretty great—harmless at worst and downright empowering at best! What could be wrong with focusing on positive things? What's the harm in believing that if we train our minds hard enough, the things, circumstances, and plans we want will come to pass?

The allure is undeniable, probably because there's some truth mixed in. Doesn't it sound like good advice to dwell on the positive rather than the negative? Doesn't it seem obviously profitable to go after the good things we want in life?

Here's the stark reality: Satan and this fallen world love to mask death, destruction, and lies as something beautiful and empowering. But the truth is, these beliefs and ideas are far from beneficial or harmless. On the contrary, dear friend, they are seriously dangerous to our souls.

Where It All Began

I remember scrolling on Instagram about a year ago and coming across a carousel post, which included multiple slides that were revealed as you swiped your finger to the left. In the middle of my mindless scroll, this post caught my eye. The first slide said something like this (I'm paraphrasing): "You have control over your life. It's time to take it." My index finger flipped to the left, and I scanned the next quote: "If you have positive thoughts and attitudes, you can manifest the life you want, and it will come to pass." The longer I read, the queasier my stomach became. With a sense of curiosity but also horror, I swiped once more to read the last quote: "You are the director, the creator, and the writer of your story. It's up to you to sit down and navigate to where you want to go and you will get there."

Why did such seemingly good and empowering quotes leave my stomach queasy? Why did they horrify me instead of pump me up with all the girl-boss vibes? Because, friend, I had spent most of my life believing the ideas presented in those quotes. Now, I may have not said those exact phrases word for word, but my actions reinforced my pride, as well as my misunderstanding of the gospel, the true calling for the Christian, and even my Savior Himself. Before God confronted me in my dorm room and challenged me to look down at my fists, my life had been directed by a false sense of reality—the same reality that those quotes promoted.

Although I accepted Jesus and became a Christian at a young age, somewhere along the line there was a disconnect. Between the world's influence and my natural, sinful instinct, my life reflected a philosophy similar to the one authors like Blavatsky preached: humanity's ability to manifest, control, and bring about whatever *they* want in their lives, without any limitations or risk of disappointment. A false sense of pride, control, and self-sufficiency had grown, and in turn, my ability to trust God had been neglected.

Although you and I may not share the same exact story, you may have already found something to relate to from my experience. You see, this isn't just a problem for the type A planners, organizers, and control freaks. Incessantly striving to control our lives and ultimately failing to trust God is a *human* problem. It's a *sin* problem. So in order to fully understand this, let's go back to where it all began.

Let's consider Adam and Eve together. In the first few chapters of the Bible, God created the world. And He created Adam and Eve for each other, for cultivating the land, and for relationship with Himself. He had laid out the perfect ecosystem. The only thing God asked of His creation, Adam and Eve, was that they not eat from the Tree of Knowledge of Good and Evil (Genesis 2:16–17). And we know how this story ends, right?

The crafty serpent took advantage of the situation and tempted Eve to question God's word. Cunningly, the serpent rephrased God's positive command and presented it in a negative way. The beauty was that God had provided everything Adam and Eve needed, and they were called to live in complete trust, believing in His provision and His word. Eating from the Tree of Knowledge of Good and Evil meant turning away from trusting in God and choosing instead to rely on their own wisdom and power. But the serpent twisted the situation. He got them to focus on the one thing God seemed to be withholding from them, instead of focusing on all the good He had given them. Instead of being thankful that God had provided everything they needed, Eve began to question why God didn't give them everything, full stop.

In the blink of an eye, the serpent had singlehandedly gotten Eve to doubt God and question His word. He exposed Eve's incomplete understanding of God's commands. Finally, it was time for the kill shot. In Genesis 3:4–5, "The serpent said to the woman, 'You will not surely die. For God knows that when you eat of it your eyes will be opened, and you will be like God, knowing good and evil.'"

The wheels in Eve's head started spinning. The more she thought about the serpent's words, the more she wanted to eat the fruit. The more enticing and delicious it looked. The more she wanted to take hold of authority and knowledge reserved only for God. The more she wanted to take control. Not long after Eve's deception, Adam also believed the lies that were planted in Eve's heart. It must have all happened so fast—first, a seemingly harmless conversation with a snake, then a bite of the fruit, then the opening of their eyes, and then disaster. The fall. The dawn of sin.

For the first time in their entire existence, Adam and Eve felt guilt. They noticed their nakedness and felt ashamed. They felt the weight of sin, evil, and death to their very core. Their eyes were opened like the serpent said, but not in a good way. Oh, how they must have thought that they would be enlightened, all powerful and in control after that bite. But instead, they were exposed to the consequences: death and a fractured relationship with God.

When I was little, I used to read the first few chapters of Genesis and become mad at Adam and Eve for what they had done to me—what they had done to all of humanity with one bite, with one decision. I would ask the questions, "How could they have been so stupid? Why didn't they trust God—their literal Creator and Father? Was Eden and perfection not good enough for them?"

As the years have passed, the Lord has convicted me of this truth: We are all like Adam and Eve. We are all easily tempted and distracted by the Enemy and the flashy things of this world. And just like Adam and Eve, we all desire to take matters into our own hands. Before the fruit was eaten from the off-limits tree, God had set up a perfect ecosystem—one where Adam and Eve were perfectly reliant upon the Lord, perfectly positioned to trust His commands. There was no such thing as sin or brokenness, so they had the ability to perfectly trust God. Before Adam and Eve sank their teeth into the fruit, there was no bone in their body that desired to take control of their lives. Why would they? They saw God for who He truly was and had no reason to question His commands or road map for their lives.

You know, we could sit here all day and complain about what Adam and Eve did when they bit into the apple, but we know that the story doesn't end there. We saw what happened when flawed individuals try to take control, direct their own paths, and not trust their loving Father. But we also see that although Adam and

Eve took control and brought a curse on humanity, God so loved the world that He gave His one and only Son (John 3:16–17). We see that in His loving-kindness, God immediately set a grand rescue story in motion for humanity through His Son, Jesus. And just as Jesus was sent to follow and trust His Father's plan above His own, so we are also called to forsake our need for control and surrender to the One who gave us life.

Addicted to Control

I'm sure you've heard stories about the effects of illicit drugs. Maybe you've seen firsthand the damage they can do in the life of a loved one or even in your very own life. Although there's a laundry list of negative side effects, such as brain damage and disease, drugs can be powerfully addictive both psychologically and physically. Surges of dopamine reward the brain, training it to seek the next high. And the longer drugs are taken, the less the mind and body are capable of resisting the temptation, despite the damage. The very thing that's poisoning the drug user seems attractive and beneficial.

Social media can be addictive for similar reasons, providing dopamine hits and training certain patterns of thoughts and behavior. And we all know that other things—like fame, money, and success—can also be addictive. But I believe that the myth of control is an especially dangerous, addictive, and universally tempting drug. It's dangerous because it masquerades as something it's not.

Some may say that being in control or wanting to be in control is natural. That if it's *our* life and future, then we have the right to take control. Others may say that control is just another word for planning—being organized and forward-thinking. I remember thinking that my intense, planner-loving, type A heart was just that—that the reason I was so set on planning my life's outcome was because I cared about my future. Those who said things like, "Oh well, it's God's timing" often rubbed me the wrong way. (Can someone say red flag?) How could people not care about their lives enough to take some action and control to ensure it all panned out? But in all reality, I had bitten into the same piece of fruit that Adam and Eve ate in the garden. I had traded in God's beautiful design for my life for the forbidden fruit of control. It looked promising, but ultimately it separated me from God and His perfect plan.

A Better Way

Our heavenly Father saw this problem coming from miles away. Way before the fall in Genesis 3, God knew you and I would have the tendency to want to swipe the pen, forsake the story He was writing, and start writing our own.

From Genesis to Revelation, we read about humanity's tendency to turn away from God and take matters into their own hands—and the tragic consequences that inevitably follow. One of Adam's sons, Cain, was possessed by jealousy and sought to control a situation that had gone awry, culminating in the murder of his own brother (Genesis 4). The people of Babel craved control and power over their own destinies and built a tower to the skies, only to be divided and scattered by God (Genesis 11). In Exodus the Israelites who were so graciously liberated from slavery by God through Moses almost immediately abandoned their divine rescuer in favor of empty idols (Exodus 32). Jonah refused to minister to Nineveh when God called him and tried his very best to edit God's master plan, only to find himself in the belly of a great fish (Jonah 1).

These were all people who knew God, who had seen His goodness and power to save, who had every reason to trust Him. But they *still* tried to grab control for themselves. Have you been there before? Have you told yourself that you trust God with your life but in the same breath turned around and insisted on your own way? Have you struggled to hold on to control, only to be left feeling defeated and frustrated with God when your plans didn't pan out? I think we all have. I know I have.

But here's the good news. Here's the beauty among the ashes, the hope among the chaos. You and I were never meant to have control over our lives—even if your plan and dream seems to have your name all over it. You and I are not powerful enough or good enough to direct our lives. Yes, friend—that *is* good news, though it might seem like a hard pill to swallow. Why? Because—let's be honest with ourselves for a moment here—we are utterly hopeless without God. We are sinful human beings. We were designed from the very beginning to need God. We were created from the ground up to depend on Him. Because of the gospel, we are not only saved from the consequences of sin but restored to a chance to live according to that beautiful, original plan—trusting and depending on our loving Father. That's what makes our neediness such unexpected good news—God Himself is our sufficiency, and He loves us enough to write a better story than we ever could.

I mean, think about it: Isn't it a blessing that we don't *have* to control our lives? That we don't have to toil, run ourselves ragged, and frustrate ourselves day in and day out? That we actually have God Himself as our designer, and that He gave us the beautiful gifts of *surrender* and *trust*? It has taken me my entire life to learn this biblical truth—that I was never created to be in control, and that's actually a beautiful thing.

But may I tell you a secret? I still struggle with opening my clenched fists and releasing the control that belongs only to my heavenly Father. Every time I start to close my fists and vie for control, I'm reminded of this truth in Proverbs 16:9, where King Solomon wrote, "The heart of man plans his way, but the LORD establishes his steps." Even the world's wisest man attempted to write his own story, under the faulty perception that he was in control. But God showed him the truth—that there was only one Lord. William McKane said this about Solomon's revelation: "A man may plan his road to the last detail, but he cannot implement his planning, unless it coincides with Yahweh's plan for him."[2]

Planning isn't a sin. A desire to strategize and look forward to our future isn't a bad thing. The error, however, is when we dig our heels in and fight for personal control over our stories instead of trusting God. What happens then is we, consciously or subconsciously, set ourselves up as lord when there is only one true Lord. Life instantly becomes more about what we want to do as the masters of our own fate rather than following our heavenly Father's will.

It may be easy to hear all of this and assume that God is bossy or rude to ask His children to give up their plans for His. But that couldn't be further from the truth. It is impossible for God to do anything that does not come from love. The Lord of lords, our Father and friend, has given us everything through his Son, Jesus (2 Peter 1:3). When we didn't deserve mercy, He poured it out—relentlessly and in overflowing excess. Instead of leaving us to fend for ourselves, He stepped in. There was a need and He filled it. Jesus' entire mission and gospel was centered on being a better sacrifice—not the temporary, partial solution that animal sacrifice provided under Old Testament law, but a complete, lasting sacrifice. Not only was He Himself the better and lasting sacrifice, but He also came to *give* a better and lasting *life* to humanity. John 10:10 says, "I came that they may have life and have it abundantly."

A life is nothing without the purpose and plans of the Lord. The full life that Jesus promises in John 10 does not come from you and me grasping at control. It does not come from us insisting on our own way. The full, abundant life available in Christ comes from surrendering our story at the foot of the cross. It comes by way of realizing our need for someone greater to write our story because we were not created to do it on our own. And if you ask me, that's pretty beautiful.

In the pages ahead I'll continue sharing parts of my story—the good and the bad. My prayer is that my vulnerability will help you reckon with the myth of control and walk your own path toward surrender. Just a heads-up: it's not an easy, linear journey, but it is a beautiful one with so much to look forward to in the future, because we know who holds our story. I have wrestled again and again with relinquishing my death grip on control, and still do to this day. But stick with me, because along the way we'll also be unpacking some key events and concepts from Scripture that will help you embrace a vital truth: when we surrender to God, it might *feel* like

> THE FULL, ABUNDANT LIFE AVAILABLE IN CHRIST COMES FROM SURRENDERING OUR STORY AT THE FOOT OF THE CROSS.

we're making a sacrifice—after all, it feels like we're being asked to give up quite a lot! But genuine surrender actually involves an awesome trade. You get to trade away the burdens of performance, legalism, and control, and instead receive what I can only describe as profound peace, real joy, and a deeply satisfying purpose. The best is yet to come when we surrender.

If you're weary, frustrated, and disappointed by your attempts to control your own story and you're ready to try the better way—then this book is for you.

Space to Surrender

Many are the plans in the mind of a man,
 but it is the purpose of the LORD that will stand.
PROVERBS 19:21

1. What are some areas in your life that God is calling you to loosen your grip on and give up some of the control you've been holding on to?
2. How have you seen God's faithfulness when you've surrendered your story to Him in the past?
3. What is one way that you can practice relinquishing control to God in your day-to-day? Maybe you borrow from my example and open your hands in prayer—or journal three to five things each day that you are thankful for here and now.

Lord, thank You for providing the perfect plan for my life. Help me to bust the myth that I am in control of my story and surrender each detail to You, the Creator and Author.

CHAPTER 2

The Freedom of Surrender

Life as a Christ follower will always be a
learning process of depending less on our
own strength and more on God's power.

LYSA TERKEURST

HEARING GOD'S VOICE IN MY biology lecture wasn't the
first time I'd wrestled with the myth of control. There's an entire
backstory, and for me to tell you that story, we need to go back
ten years. Lean in, friend. This story is so important because it
reveals how learning to surrender isn't a onetime event. It's a

lifelong pursuit, but not one without hope and the promise of a brighter, more fulfilling purpose than we could ever dream for ourselves.

It was Memorial Day weekend. My sleepy eyes slowly fluttered open as I woke to the sound of waves crashing on the Oregon coast. For as long as I could remember, my family and our best friends would spend that entire weekend together at their beach house—eating delicious food, walking the beach, climbing the sand dunes, and just taking time to be.

I had just turned fourteen that January. That year was especially significant to me because it meant it was finally time to move on to high school. Growing up in a small, sheltered middle school, my heart was aching to escape that bubble and embrace something new. I was ready for bigger classes, Friday night football games, a little more independence, and the high school experience. (Who am I kidding? I was fourteen. I was probably just excited about the boys.)

Freshman orientation was scribbled in bright, bold letters on my calendar. Summer couldn't come fast enough because it meant that with each passing day, high school got a little bit closer. But then, amid the excitement and anticipation, the unexpected happened. A ginormous wrench was thrown in my perfect plan.

When my eyes opened that morning, I could not move. And then my body was frozen in all shapes and sizes of pain.

There I lay in bed, simultaneously listening to the peaceful sound of the waves and experiencing the worst horror and pain I had ever felt. After a few minutes of struggling, I used every ounce of strength, flung my arm across the bed, and grabbed my phone to text my mom upstairs.

"Mom, something's wrong. Please come here."

Not Part of the Plan

My feet dangled off the doctor's examination table, nervously kicking as I waited for the results of my lab work to come back. It was a few months after the incident at the beach, and during that time my family and I had relentlessly sought doctor after doctor, specialist after specialist. Needless to say, my grand aspirations for my first year of high school did not quite go according to my plan.

Instead of walking down the halls to Algebra 1 with new friends, I lay limp in my bedroom, writhing in pain. Instead of joining my classmates in Friday night football cheers and getting invited to parties, social anxiety and depression grew in my heart because of the isolation that resulted from the constant pain. My family and I made the hard decision to withdraw me from my first year of high school. The sobering truth was that I just could not go to school. Not because I was not academically prepared. Not because I was afraid of being the new girl. But because my body had contracted a mysterious illness, and we had no idea where it came from, what it was, or how to combat it.

After what seemed like hours of waiting, the pediatric specialist walked back into my examination room, his face expressionless. My parents and I sat there in silence as he went on to explain that I had fibromyalgia, or amplified pain syndrome (AMPS), as they call it in children and young adults. I remember holding back the tears from pouring out of my eyes as I heard him tell me what it all meant.

The doctor went on to explain that a mononucleosis virus "awoke" this fibromyalgia beast inside of me. This is a chronic condition that usually plagues middle-aged individuals, but every once in a while, it finds younger patients like me. AMPS is characterized by episodes, or flare-ups, of pain that can come in two sizes: intermittent or constant.

Think about this: What would happen if you stepped on a tack? The pain in your foot sends a signal through the nerve to your spinal cord. From there, the signal is transferred to the brain. Finally, the brain recognizes the pain signal and your body goes into all sorts of reactions. But when it comes to AMPS, there is an abnormal short circuit in the spinal cord. The normal pain signal travels up to the brain but *also* goes to the neurovascular nerves. These nerves are known as the "fight or flight" nerves. Something happens with these nerves to also affect the blood vessels, which causes a buildup of lactic acid in the muscles, resulting in widespread pain.

And as you can imagine, the cycle I've described just continues. On and on and on. As if there is an error code going off in my body or a wire that is not connected properly.

My mom asked the doctor, "What are our next steps? What does treatment and recovery look like for this illness?"

He paused and took a few glances at my parents and then at me.

"Fibromyalgia is a chronic illness. It may never go away for you, Tara. Some people do go into remission, and they do not have to deal with it for the rest of their lives. Then there are some who fight it their whole lives. But either way, there is therapy and next steps we can take."

The following months were miserable, to say the least. It felt as if I was climbing uphill with two boulders attached at my hips, weighing me down the mountain on a blistering, 175-degree day. Oh, and it also felt like I was blindfolded and tripping with each step.

The game plan was physical and occupational therapy a few times a week up north. Each time, my mom would drag me out of bed, and we would drive an hour both directions for the sessions. At this point my attitude was less than ideal. Granted, I was in excruciating pain and barely able to get out of bed most days. Honestly, walking ten steps from my bed to my bathroom was a strenuous ordeal.

It probably comes as no surprise that fourteen-year-old Tara was the sourest Sour Patch Kid in the box. She looked on her doctor's orders with contempt and pushback because her body hurt so bad. She cried and yelled at her parents when they gently asked her to get ready for therapy because all she wanted to do was lie in bed and feel sorry for herself. She secluded herself from her friends and peers because she was afraid of what people thought of her now that she was "disabled." She yelled and screamed at God until her eyes and throat were swollen because it felt like God had deserted her. It was as if God didn't care about her, because all of a sudden, her future seemed crushed and ruined.

Although I had accepted Christ at a young age and had been given a "new flesh" in Him, my old flesh still fought back. The excruciating pain that wreaked havoc on my body was not relenting, nor did it seem like it would anytime soon. So what happened, you ask? My fists clenched down harder and tighter. My knuckles turned purple. Amid these circumstances, instead of seeing all of it as an opportunity to trust God and build my faith, I saw it as an opportunity to blame God. I saw it as an opportunity to live in denial—pretending that my plans for high school, my future career, my relationships, and life in general were still up to me. That although I had hit a temporary roadblock, I still had control and I could still navigate back onto the Highway of Tara. Even though life had clearly just been flipped upside down, there was still a huge part of my heart that was not ready to release that death grip on control.

But after completing the first few months of physical therapy and adjusting to a new set of circumstances, I finally started to face reality. The Portland doctor's diagnosis replayed over and over in my ears: *This may be a lifelong journey of dealing with this illness.* Every movement in physical therapy was sobering, making me realize that my plans for my life were slowly fading away. Every moment I lay in bed with mind-numbing pain was a stark reminder that my plan had been derailed. As I missed more and more school and the life experiences I'd so been looking forward to, I started to face the facts: I was not in control.

I continued to struggle with bitterness, but my controlling heart slowly began to soften. My death grip began to relax. My bullheaded stubbornness to fight and control the outcome of my life started to disintegrate. God let me come to the end of myself, and I started to experience something I didn't expect—a newfound freedom. It was the kind of freedom that made me realize I did not have to hustle and run myself completely empty trying to achieve the perfect outcome for my life—because God had a better plan, even if it didn't make sense to me in the moment.

It seems backward or upside-down, doesn't it? You'd think that experiencing freedom in our lives would be all about having control over the direction and outcome of every little thing. But it's actually when we surrender that we find the freedom, peace, and purpose we have been searching for our entire lives.

An Upside-Down Kingdom

A few years ago, my pastor started a sermon series called "Upside-Down Kingdom" that walked, verse by verse, through the Gospel of Matthew. The moment he announced the title, my jaw dropped a little.

Upside-down kingdom?

The word *kingdom* is popular in Christian churches and circles, but the upside-down part really threw me for a loop that Sunday morning. I will never forget Pastor Stan opening his Bible and saying, "Jesus came to bring an upside-down kingdom to a world that was right side up. As we will learn in our study of Matthew, Jesus' life and ministry was actually upside down."

Let's put our thinking caps on together for a moment: What does it mean for something to be upside down? My mind immediately rushes to the thought of someone hanging upside down from a roller coaster—shoes above their heads, suspended hundreds of feet in the air.

You may be wondering, *How can you say that Jesus was backward or out of order? Isn't that kind of offensive to say about God Almighty?*

Yes, Jesus is God incarnate. Yes, He is perfect and without flaw. But here's the thing: to many of the people He came to save, Jesus was upside down. His philosophies were upside down. His teachings were countercultural and, at first glance, confusing. Jesus' ideas often seemed topsy-turvy.

First Corinthians 2:14 says, "The natural person does not accept the things of the Spirit of God, for they are folly to him, and he is not able to understand them because they are spiritually discerned." Paul, the author of 1 Corinthians, used the phrase "natural person" to describe people who were living solely for the here and now—as if there was nothing beyond this physical life. The crazy thing is that all humans are natural persons at the start of their lives. As I mentioned earlier, we were born with a sin nature. But when the grace of God appeared through Jesus

Christ, we were given the opportunity to receive the free gift of salvation. When we put our faith in Jesus, we are given a new life, a new nature, and a new operating system.

No wonder people considered Jesus and His teachings to be upside down. Although many people believed and loved and followed Him, a great majority were not able to understand Jesus' life and ministry because their operating systems were old and outdated. They needed new operating systems—regenerated hearts to understand the things of the Spirit. The same goes for the world we live in now.

> WHEN WE PUT OUR FAITH IN JESUS, WE ARE GIVEN A NEW LIFE, A NEW NATURE, AND A NEW OPERATING SYSTEM.

If we take an honest look at Jesus' life and what He preached, we're faced with lots of shocking and upside-down things. Many, if not all, of Jesus' sermons and commandments were out of the norm and sometimes offensive to the prevailing culture. Growing up, I tended to see Jesus as the loving King up in the clouds where sunshine, rainbows, and unicorns danced. Everything I knew about Him (which, at that time, was not much at all) was easy for me. I simply focused on Jesus being loving, caring, and compassionate.

And although those things are true about our Savior, I was missing a very important piece of the puzzle: Jesus was offensive. Now, I do not mean that He was disrespectful, insulting, or out to stir up controversy and incite riots. But the words and truths that Jesus built His kingdom upon tended to ruffle feathers. Why? Because they went against humanity's sin nature. They weren't easy things to do or easy commandments to get up and follow.

24

From the moment Jesus was born, He was not quite what the world was expecting from a Messiah. The Jews were expecting a powerful king, praised and accepted by all. They were expecting Him to be the center of attention and come bursting onto the scene with some big, grand gesture. Perhaps they were expecting their Messiah to come crashing through the city with a loud voice and flashy campaign and decked out in the most impressive attire. In the Jews' minds, their long-awaited Savior and Messiah would be obvious in all grandeur.

But Jesus smashed those expectations. He was an upside-down king, bringing a beautiful, upside-down kingdom. His virgin mother gave birth to Him in a dusty, stinky stable. A feeding trough was His crib.

Jesus was raised as a humble carpenter with "no beauty that we should desire him" (Isaiah 53:2). Outwardly, He was likely unimpressive. Seemingly normal. Contrary to what the world would expect of a powerful king, Jesus did not keep company with the most noble and powerful people. His core group consisted of twelve misfits—fishermen, a frowned-upon tax collector, extremists, and so on. Although thousands of people flocked to listen to Him, you would not find Jesus up on a stage in a sold-out arena for hundreds of thousands. In fact, you could often find Jesus sitting cross-legged on the grass among the poor or sitting on a rock by the sea.

Jesus came to bring change. He came to offer His people a better, surpassing way to live through His gift of salvation. And the cornerstone of that better way of life is found in one of the most shocking verses of all time:

And he said to all, "If anyone would come after me, let him deny himself and take up his cross daily and follow me. For whoever would save his life will lose it, but whoever loses his life for my sake will save it. For what does it profit a man if he gains the whole world and loses or forfeits himself?" (Luke 9:23–25)

Truth be told, when I first read this passage as a new Christian, I found it super unsettling. The idea of denying ourselves and taking up our crosses was scary. The idea of losing our lives to save them sounded like a complete oxymoron. It all sounded like Jesus was asking the disciples (and us, because this truth is for all of us as well) to give up their lives. To just become robots and stop enjoying life or having fun.

But as I began digging, I discovered that being a disciple required three things:

1. To deny ourselves,
2. To take up our crosses,
3. To follow Him.

Jesus is not interested in lukewarm disciples. He is interested in people who choose Him above themselves and their own comfort.

Denying ourselves means more than denying ourselves certain things or products or lifestyles; it means letting go of personal control of our lives. Just as we learned about Adam and Eve, humanity has always struggled with a desire to overthrow the sovereign power of God in exchange for their own.

When Jesus said these challenging words to His disciples, He wasn't being harsh or cruel. He did not ask these men to die to themselves because He wanted to see them suffer. On the contrary! This was the new, redemptive way of life that God was ushering into the world through His Son, searching the world for true disciples that would count the cost of following Him and see that it was good. God was looking for disciples who believed the surrender was worth it in exchange for a beautiful relationship, a promising future, and the hope of heaven.

The same goes for you and me. When our heavenly Father asks us to die to ourselves, He is asking us to trust Him. He is asking us to unclench our fists, open up our hands, and rest in His grace. Self-denial feels like a sacrifice and a stretch at first—but it's actually an invitation to lay down the burden of control and experience the gift of faith and trust in God. Self-denial allows us to experience His tender love over our lives.

Second, Jesus asks us to take up our crosses. When we think of the word *cross*, we usually are taken back to the brutal execution that Jesus endured for us on Calvary. We picture a wood cross covered by the blood of our Savior. But this call to take up our crosses really means to make a commitment. It's a metaphor for being prepared to face whatever may come, just as Jesus did for us. It means putting Him ahead of our own comfort and safety.

Being a disciple of Christ requires fierce commitment—a desire to be "all in" for God. No sitting on the fence. And taking up your cross isn't a once-and-done situation. Do you remember what Jesus said? "Let him deny himself and take up his cross *daily* and follow me" (v. 23, emphasis added).

Are we willing to commit to following the Lord *daily*? Are we willing to die for the sake of Christ? Are we willing to be laughed at for His sake? Rejected or "canceled" by society, our friends, or even our families?

Last, Jesus asks His people to follow Him—to imitate His example and obey His teaching. When Jesus said, "follow me,"

He meant joining the company of His disciples. Simply put, Jesus concluded this hard but beautiful mini sermon by challenging us to look to Him for guidance and to fellowship in His company. To not grow weary but to find our strength, example, and life in Him. To wake up every day with a desire to live like Him.

After reading this passage for the first time, I shook my head. I felt completely in over my head. It felt like I was staring at an overwhelming mountain of a task. Perhaps you've been reading this chapter with me and felt the same things. You might be thinking, *Tara, the cross feels too heavy. Letting go of control and denying myself every day . . . I don't think I can do it. Not to mention Jesus is* perfect. *How could I ever follow His example?*

Rest for Your Soul

In Matthew 11:29–30 Jesus spoke these tender and comforting words: "Take my yoke upon you, and learn from me, for I am gentle and lowly in heart, and you will find rest for your souls. For my yoke is easy, and my burden is light."

In the New Testament the Pharisees were a bunch of "Legalistic Larrys." Everything they did came from a place of merely checking off a list because they were "supposed to" and because it made them "look good"—not because they truly loved God or desired to follow Him. In Matthew 11 Jesus was calling those who felt burdened by the overwhelming weight of these legalistic requirements. Jesus was calling those who were tired of carrying their own burdens and trying to meet every expectation through their own strength.

Our gentle and lowly Savior has a solution for those who are weary and burdened. A yoke was a tool used to join two animals together so they could work in unison and share the load of pulling a plow or a cart. Humanity's tendency to live out of obligation and strive for their own worth was only crushing them. But Jesus' yoke of discipleship—this idea of denying ourselves, taking up our crosses, and following Him—brings rest and freedom.

Let Jesus' promise be your guarantee: We do not have to be afraid to be disciples of Christ. We do not have to be overwhelmed by what Jesus calls us to. We do not have to worry about what we will lose when we surrender our lives, release personal control, take up our crosses, and follow Jesus instead. We have a Savior who has extended His hand down from heaven and offered us salvation. In Christ we have victory. We have the win. We have the ultimate gain, not loss. We do not have to strive and control and plan and manipulate to reach victory, because Jesus has already won it on our behalf.

WE DO NOT HAVE TO STRIVE AND CONTROL AND PLAN AND MANIPULATE TO REACH VICTORY, BECAUSE JESUS HAS ALREADY WON IT ON OUR BEHALF.

Sure, we have the option to go about living our lives trying to white-knuckle our way to success and achievement. But as Luke 9:25 asks, what's the point of gaining the whole world only to lose ourselves in the process? Whatever we might win for ourselves is infinitely less valuable than the eternal purpose and destiny available in God. What we see now and what the world offers—fame, money, success, external achievements—is far less satisfying than what God has for us.

God does not want you to run yourself ragged. He does not want to see you suffer through clenched fists, broken dreams, and disappointment. If you remember anything from this chapter, remember this: Jesus may have said a lot of upside-down things in His lifetime. He may have ruffled a lot of feathers and said things that sent people into shock. But He did it to make beautiful, committed, and holy disciples out of you and me. He did it to change the game and offer something far better than the world could offer. His teachings only seem upside down because our world is upside down. Ever since the fall, we've been fighting with ourselves, with each other, and with the world around us, trying to grab control and impose our will on our circumstances. Jesus' invitation to deny ourselves, pick up our crosses, and follow Him is actually an invitation to lay down the burden of sinfully trying to control our own lives, and instead, pick up His gift of true grace, freedom, and rest.

When Jesus has your heart, your desires, and your affections, you're returning to the kind of connection with God that you were created for. There is a greater purpose and plan for our lives when we wave our white flags and say, "Lord, I surrender. I am tired of striving. I am tired of holding on to control. I want a life that is full of freedom and purpose. I want to be Your disciple."

And rest assured, my friend: God isn't asking us to release our control so He can "bait and switch" us. He is not out to trick us. We don't have to worry about being left empty-handed. On the contrary. When our heavenly Father asks us to give up something, He always has something exceedingly better in store.

Space to Surrender

Take my yoke upon you, and learn from me, for I am gentle and lowly in heart, and you will find rest for your souls. For my yoke is easy, and my burden is light.

MATTHEW 11:29-30

1. Do you have trouble surrendering *all*? Or are some things easier to relinquish than others? Why do you think that is?
2. Reflect on how the three steps to discipleship—deny yourself, take up your cross, follow Jesus—make you feel. What emotions does this stir: fear, anxiety, courage, hope?
3. How does seeing God's kingdom through the "upside-down" lens change your perspective on your story and help you trust Him more?

Heavenly Father, thank You for taking on my burdens and releasing me from striving for my worth. I pray that You would help me to deny myself, take up my cross, and follow You every single day. Help me to walk in the freedom and rest that only You offer through surrender.

CHAPTER 3

Independence Is Overrated

I have a great need for Christ; I have
a great Christ for my need.
CHARLES SPURGEON

THUD.

The last box of my belongings hit the floor. My eyes misted with tears as my parents retreated down the stairs to give me some time alone. With a heavy sigh, I slumped down on my bed and scanned the room. *This is my new reality—I had better get used to it.*

I had just officially become a college dropout and moved back to my childhood home with my parents. My bed, desk, and every inch of the floor were covered in clothes, toiletries, desk supplies, and school materials I had lugged home from college.

It had been two weeks since God had told me, *Tara, you're not supposed to be here*, in the middle of my biology lecture. The days after this revelation were exactly what you would imagine them to be. My body and spirit felt numb, confused, and weary. I would go out with friends and do the normal college thing, but even my somewhat convincing fake smile couldn't hide the fact that I was in turmoil. I mustered up the courage to attend my classes, but now I felt a dull sense of purposelessness, as I wondered, *What's the use?*

It was at this point that I couldn't deny it any longer. I pulled out my phone and called my parents and boyfriend, Michael, to tell them what had happened—that my world and plans had been sent into a tailspin. My parents' first reaction was shock, panic, and confusion—understandable, right? My boyfriend, although excited by the potential that we wouldn't have to do long-distance anymore, wondered out loud, "Tara, are you sure?"

His question lingered in my mind. Was I *really* sure? Was that *really* God speaking?

A few days later, I woke up to my phone alarm only to realize that my body was pulsing. I groaned, turned over, and threw my pillow over my head. The feeling was unmistakable. I was having a fibromyalgia flare-up. My head felt as if it was splitting and every muscle in my body was on fire. Little did I know that this flare-up would last all week. Little did I know that I would end up going back to my childhood home to rest and recover. And little did I know that those days weren't just to recover but for God to give me the answers I was desperate for.

The time spent on my parents' couch recovering that week provided the perfect opportunity to be still. To wrestle with God. To patiently wait for His clarity on this most confusing situation. To get perspective and counsel from the people I loved and trusted. In the following days, after bingeing on ice cream, praying, and exhausting my tear supply, the fog began to lift. God brought me the gift of clarity about my situation. And He revived my weary body. The lingering questions—*Is this really God speaking?* and *Am I really not supposed to be here?*—were met with His answers.

God's answer was *yes* in all caps. *Yes* in bright neon letters. *Yes* over the loudspeakers. But while I felt relieved to finally have an answer from God, it didn't mean that the next part came easy. It wasn't easy to explain to my college friends and family that I was dropping out within the first month of starting. It wasn't easy to say that my dreams and aspirations of going to a great university and becoming a doctor were suddenly over. I felt embarrassed and ashamed to pack up my belongings and just disappear. And I definitely didn't feel great about moving back home with my parents without a clear next step in place.

So there I found myself, back in my tiny room. I'd traded three roommates and a lively college scene for solitude. I'd exchanged the excitement and purpose of college classes, five-year plans, and the prospect of medical school applications for feeling completely directionless. Now, you would think that after God's clear answer and confirmation I would be at His beck and call. You would think that after God made it obvious He had something else for me, I would just wait patiently for Him to show me what was next.

But surprise, surprise. Instead of surrendering to God and waiting on Him to tell me *His* next step, I took *my* next step. As I adjusted to a new schedule back at home, I occupied my mind with thoughts of *my* next thing instead of *God's* next thing. Instead of releasing my death grip on control, I packed up my lunch bag each day and headed off to work for myself as the CEO of self-sufficiency. I started hustling and planning to get my life back on track as quickly as possible. And I was definitely looking for ways to skip over the whole waiting-on-God process.

The days following my embarrassing college dropout experience typically looked like this: My alarm clock would ring at 7:00 A.M. sharp, and I would make my way downstairs. The house was quiet, with only the sound of my parents flipping the pages of their Bibles in the family room. The pellet stove gently hummed as the Oregon fall colors began to show that October. I would grab a bowl of yogurt and granola, pour my cup of coffee, and top it with foam. Then I would shuffle back to my room.

After finishing the last delicious bites of yogurt, I'd cuddle up in my warm sheets and grab my Bible off the nightstand, flip to the book of the Bible I was working through, and read. That may sound cozy and perfect on the surface, but deep down inside, I felt numb and cold—not just to my situation or my day-to-day life, but to my heavenly Father.

Begrudgingly, I did the "Christian thing." I "put Jesus first," as the popular saying goes, making sure I marked "read your Bible" off my planner. I wanted so badly to believe that I was in the center of God's will, that His plan of pulling me from college and giving me a chronic illness was all for His good purpose. A plan not to harm me but to give me a future, right? (Remember Jeremiah 29:11.) And yet I couldn't help feeling that I had been duped, that God had somehow let me down.

Now, I would argue that all parents hope their children will grow up to be independent. Their prayers may include something about them becoming strong and capable on their own, because the reality is that child won't be under their roof forever. That's exactly how I was raised, too, and there's nothing wrong with that. Not only am I a natural type A planner and organizer, but I was also raised as a farm kid. Each summer my brother, cousins, and I would work on the family hazelnut farm. It was hard, sweaty work that involved lifting, digging, pruning, running a tractor, and more. From a young age, I prided myself on the personal strength and determination I had (and which my parents had definitely fostered).

That was what I was going to do in this new season. I was going to get up, regain my independence, and take back control of my life.

So after checking off my Bible reading in my daily planner, I spent my waking hours applying to any and every job I could think of. Googling into the wee hours of the night, looking for a new career idea that might pique my interest. Not long after, I found myself with a seasonal retail job at my local Nordstrom store. I thought, "Okay, maybe this is it. Maybe I've found it." There was nothing wrong with being diligent and getting back to life after God's redirection. It was actually a good thing I did not sit around and twiddle my thumbs (Proverbs 10:4). But the error of my ways was assuming I could find God's will for my life on my own. It was easier to listen to and follow myself instead of waiting on God to show me the sure way. And inevitably, the Christmas season came and went, with Nordstrom failing to hire me back.

But a few months later, I secured another retail job. This time I was working at Anthropologie. I was the girl you would find on the floor, refolding clothes, steaming new arrivals, opening dressing rooms, and ringing you up at the counter. At one point I finally hit an anniversary of sorts—the major retail seasons came and went, and I still had a job with them. (Go me, right?) If you were to ask me in that moment if I felt like retail was God's next step for me, I most likely would have scoffed and told you, "Well, it sure seems like it. I'm still here, aren't I?"

But in reality and all honesty, it was just something to distract me from listening to God.

I was making decisions without even considering God.

I was making decisions without first being in deep prayer.

I was making decisions without stopping to even consider if it was what God wanted me to do—or just what I wanted to do.

I was under the impression that my ways were better and faster than God's.

Dependent Disciples

That nasty drug named control had worked its way back into my system, and this time it was wearing a very effective disguise. My desire to be independent seemed praiseworthy, hiding under my go-getter, hardworking attitude, but it was covering up an ugly truth: I still had a deep-rooted desire for control. I still wasn't willing to surrender my story and wait for God to direct my steps.

When I prepare to speak, record a podcast episode, or even write an Instagram caption, I like to think in what I call "opposites." Instead of immediately getting to the heart of the issue, I like to define what that issue *is not*. The benefit to thinking in opposites is that when you clearly know what something is *not*, it's easier to identify what it truly *is*.

So, as we venture deeper into this beautiful idea of surrender (yes, I promise you, it's truly beautiful), I would be remiss if I did not mention one of surrender's greatest opposites and enemies: self-sufficiency.

On the surface self-sufficiency doesn't sound half bad, right? As I mentioned earlier, most of us are raised to be independent individuals. Think back to when you were a little child. I mean, how excited were you to grow up? How excited were you to finally get past the nap stage and be able to do whatever you wanted during that time? I remember two distinct moments in my growing up years when I felt I'd reached a significant milestone on the path to independence. The first was when I finally could do a ballet bun in my own hair without my mom's help—it might sound silly, but I had very long, thick hair, so it was a real challenge to do it on my own! The second was when I got my driver's license. I had been driving tractors and my family's cars around our property for years, so it felt like a long time coming. Just hours after getting my license, I told (not asked) my dad that I was going to take a little drive up one of Oregon's busiest freeways. I turned the key in the ignition and pulled out of the driveway feeling like an absolute boss.

Now, it's not wrong to drive on your own, think on your own, or work on your own. Heck, I am one of the biggest advocates for learning how to be a hard, diligent worker and not living complacently like Proverbs 13:4 counsels. In the same vein, Colossians 3:23 encourages us to "work heartily, as for the Lord and not for men." The life of a disciple is not well lived or stewarded for God's glory if it is lived passively, carelessly, or irresponsibly.

But in Jesus' upside-down kingdom, we see there's more to the story: working diligently and being responsible is one thing. But believing we are strong enough, powerful enough, and wise enough *on our own* to live our lives apart from God is another thing.

We weren't created to be self-sufficient boss babes, but wholly *dependent* disciples.

This is one of the most countercultural messages I could share with you in today's world. In a culture saturated with messages promoting self-sufficiency and independence, God's economy and agenda sends a completely different message—one that holds the most promise, purpose, and fulfillment.

> WE WEREN'T CREATED TO BE SELF-SUFFICIENT BOSS BABES, BUT WHOLLY *DEPENDENT* DISCIPLES.

Every time we buy into the lie that we are self-sufficient beings apart from God, we believe that we do not need God's empowerment or God's lordship over our lives. In Ephesians 2:8–9 Paul wanted the church at Ephesus to understand the lavish gift of God's grace. Read it with me: "For by grace you have been saved through faith. And this is not your own doing; it is the gift of God, not a result of works, so that no one may boast."

Did you catch that? The life we live and the salvation we've been given is not a result of our abilities or our own strength, but a work of God's grace. Paul couldn't have made it clearer: *It is not our own doing; it is the gift of God*. What does this tell us?

This tells us that we are completely dependent on God to save us and continue His work through us daily. Our salvation is a gift of God's own goodness, not one that we can achieve for ourselves based on our own merit, efforts, or control.

This grace is the opposite of autonomy, another way to say self-sufficiency.

Self-sufficiency tells us that we can do it on our own, that we have the power and capability within ourselves to get the job done; grace tells us God has already done it.

Self-sufficiency suggests we can declare out loud the lives we
want and see it come to pass from our own willpower;
grace reminds us that everything is a gift from God.
Self-sufficiency is a form of pride; grace is our humble
reality.

I will admit that believing I am enough on my own and falling
into pride as a consequence has been one of my biggest struggles
and sins. And yet here I am writing a book about it. That's often
how God works, am I right?

Perhaps you're just like me—type A, very organized, and very
capable, with an independent personality. Or perhaps you're more
type B—laid back, go-with-the-flow, very spur-of-the-moment.
No matter what category we fall into, we can all look to situations in our lives in which we have taken the steering wheel
away from God because we thought we were capable enough.
We thought, *I got this*, because we had a better idea of how the
story should read than God. The road we chose may not have had
too many potholes or U-turns along the way, but eventually we
could see the road lines ahead of us blurring. We could sense that
something wasn't quite right.

Why?

Because we were never created to be self-sufficient. The truth
of the matter is, God didn't wire us that way. We may stumble
along, seeming to get by okay on our own merit, but we can't
expect to *thrive*. We were fearfully and wonderfully made to be
wholly dependent disciples. And I'm here to tell you there's nothing wrong with being reliant on or sustained by God. It doesn't
make you weak; rather, it makes you strong. It releases your
chains of striving and performing. It gives you rest, knowing you
don't have to have it all together because you are held by a God

who does. It opens your eyes to a life story you never thought possible because it's not up to you; it's up to the Creator of the universe.

Now, don't take my word for it. In these next few pages, let's look together at the prime example of a life dependent upon God and see the freedom, purpose, and beauty for ourselves.

Following in His Footsteps

There was always that one kid in Sunday school. I'm sure you know who I'm talking about. He or she was the one who answered every question with "Jesus!" even if it was a question about how many animals Noah fit into the ark. I used to roll my eyes at kids like that, but now that I've gotten older, I'm realizing that maybe they were onto something.

Jesus. Simply Jesus. It all comes down to Him. The world's greatest example of someone completely and utterly dependent on God. The world's greatest example of someone who deferred to God's plan over His own. The world's greatest example of someone who didn't operate out of self-sufficiency but relinquished His own desires to serve a bigger purpose. Essentially, Jesus was just the GOAT (greatest of all time). Amen? Amen.

Now, stick with me here. I see the wheels turning in your mind. Yes, Jesus was fully God and fully man. Yes, Jesus was perfect and we are not. For those reasons we can't be *exactly* like Him. But what we can do, and what God calls us to do in the Bible, is to look at His example and imitate His life to the best of our ability. Talk about the greatest role model *ever*. The apostle Paul challenged the church at Ephesus and us to "be imitators of God, as beloved children" (Ephesians 5:1). Christians are called to emulate God's holiness. Because God has made us His children, we have the freedom and empowerment of the Holy Spirit to live a new way. And God didn't ask us to live a holy, set-apart life without providing help. He gave His Son to look to, and that's exactly what we're going to do now.

You may see Luke 22:42 written on a cute wooden sign in a friend's house or placed in someone's Instagram bio. It's the moment when Jesus prayed to God to take away His cup of suffering to come, foreshadowing when He would be separated from His Father and die a painful death on the cross. After withdrawing from His disciples and wandering off to a secluded place, He prayed honestly and vulnerably: "Father, if you are willing, remove this cup from me. Nevertheless, not my will, but yours, be done."

Can you imagine this moment? Jesus, with sweat and tears pouring out of His body, asking His Father to spare Him in a moment of weakness. He admitted His fear of what was to come and asked God if His pain could be taken away. But instead of making this request a demand, Jesus uttered the words, "Not my will, but yours, be done." Our Savior consciously, voluntarily, and obediently endured the cross for us (Hebrews 12:2). Our Savior, despite admitting His natural human fears, chose to be obedient to what God wanted Him to do. He chose wholehearted dependence on His Father over insisting on His own way.

That wasn't the only instance that Jesus chose dependence on God over independence. That dramatic, heart-wrenching episode in Gethsemane was the culmination of a lifetime of choices both big and small. Jesus' entire life, from His birth in a manger to His ascension into heaven, was under the direction of God. Think of the time when He managed to slip away from His parents as a twelve-year-old, only to be found in the temple, sitting among the teachers of the law. Shocked, angry, and perhaps even a bit impressed, His parents asked Him why He had taken off. The twelve-year-old Savior simply replied, "Why were you looking for me? Did you not know that I must be in my Father's house?" (Luke 2:49). Boom. Talk about a mic-drop moment. Even at the young age of twelve, Jesus understood His assignment. Jesus understood He was the Son of God. Jesus fully realized He wasn't in charge of His life, able to do whatever He pleased, but that everything was controlled by His heavenly Father. His priority was God and where God wanted Him to be. Now, fast-forward through the years of Jesus' life with me. Throughout the Scriptures, we read dozens of stories about Jesus' day-to-day life. We read miraculous stories of healing and deliverance. We read beautifully deep and thoughtful parables Jesus told to the few and to the thousands. But what are the common threads that bind all His actions and appointments during His thirty-three years on earth?

Dependence. Wholehearted humility. Denying His desire for control and surrendering to God's mission.

With every miracle Jesus performed, Jesus demonstrated that God's way was more important to follow than His own. With each sermon and teaching He shared, He demonstrated that He was put on earth to carry out God's will alone. With every encounter and mundane task, He demonstrated that surrender was far more precious than chasing after personal control.

It wasn't just Jesus' declaration hours before His death that earned Him the title of greatest surrenderer of all time. It wasn't just Jesus' prayer in the garden and the selfless death He died on the cross that earned Him the title of the greatest example to follow of all time. What made Him the greatest example of humility, dependence, and reliance on God was a combination of every intentional decision He made on earth. Yes, even the seemingly commonplace things like getting out of bed, having daily conversations, walking dusty roads, and working as a part-time carpenter.

And you and I, friend, have that same potential through Jesus Christ. Because He is our greatest example, because we are given the Holy Spirit when we put our trust in Him, we, too, can live out of wholehearted dependence instead of self-sufficiency.

Think about what would have happened if Jesus had chosen to go His own way. Think of what we all would have missed out on. The same goes for you and me. Take comfort in the fact that God never asks us to rely on Him without His promises and provisions. Take comfort in the fact that we are not capable or sufficient in ourselves, and that's not a bad thing. Take comfort in the fact that it's a gift not to rely on ourselves but on a heavenly Father who is far greater, wiser, and stronger.

Sure, it may be painful and confusing at times. It may feel like you're moving at a snail's pace. You may be tempted to rush ahead of God's timing. I have felt all those things and more, especially when I came home from college with no game plan. But here is the joy, here is the good news: God created us to be dependent human beings—not discounting the unique gifts and abilities He's given each one of us—so that we could be living testimonies of His strength. So that He could do abundantly, immeasurably more through us than we could do on our own.

I pray these ideas of self-sufficiency and wholehearted dependence on God have not scared you. I pray they have brought more understanding and freedom than you once imagined. I pray Jesus' gentle and inspiring example of dependence has excited you about what God can do with your surrendered heart. I pray you become a person who does not bear down on their fists, tip their nose up to the sky, and proclaim, "I can do this" in pride—but one who releases their fists, humbles their heart, and proclaims, "Not my will, but Yours be done."

I'm Not Enough, and That's Okay

I remember the last piece of clothing I folded at Anthropologie. I remember my last day working alongside my coworkers, scanning price tags, and packaging a customer's order in tissue paper. After I worked nearly a year at Anthropologie, God had made it painfully aware that I needed to move on. That I needed to stop pursuing a career in retail, because I was operating out of self-sufficiency. I was grasping at straws to make something happen in my timeline and my story and had completely forgotten His upside-down kingdom.

Dependence on Him over independence and self-sufficiency.

And as you can imagine, God started to open doors and bring clarity as I slowly learned to unclench my fists and embrace His gentle way of dependence. The doors didn't all swing open right away with a blaring sign that said, "This way!" None of it happened overnight, because frankly, that's not always how God works. Sometimes I'm tempted to think that God is aloof or disinterested in me because my prayers for clarity and direction aren't delivered in my time frame. But nothing could be further from the truth.

Oftentimes our heavenly Father uses the "not yets" of life to remind us to cling to Him harder. To depend on Him deeper. To remember who's truly in control (spoiler alert: it's not us). To realize that we truly have no other recourse than to lean on God to answer and guide us into what's next. And what humbling reminders, right?

But if we choose to look at these seasons of waiting through the lens of eternity, we will begin to see that they are all a part of God's plan—to create an intimate, dependent relationship that recognizes we aren't enough on our own, but that's okay. A relationship that recognizes we are needy people, but which doesn't make us hopeless or bad people. What it does do is make us *hope-filled* people who take full advantage of God's sufficiency instead of relying on our own.

I remember what I did after my last day working at Anthropologie. I spent some vulnerable time with the Lord in His Word. Most of it was spent questioning God, if I'm being completely honest. Through the tears, I felt the Spirit prompt me to open my Bible to 2 Corinthians. Now this wasn't a crazy ask because 2 Corinthians was one of my favorite books in the New Testament. The endless notes, highlighter scribbles, and stickers filling Paul's second letter to the church at Corinth showed just how much I loved this book.

OFTENTIMES OUR HEAVENLY FATHER USES THE "NOT YETS" OF LIFE TO REMIND US TO CLING TO HIM HARDER.

My eyes landed on chapter 3, verse 5. To my surprise, I noticed that there were no pen scribbles, underlining, or highlighting on this verse. For the girl who had grown up reading the Bible her whole life, I was shocked and intrigued. The Lord spoke these gentle words over me, and I believe God wants to speak them over you too: "Such is the confidence that we have through Christ toward God. Not that we are sufficient in ourselves to claim anything as coming from us, but our sufficiency is from God, who has made us sufficient to be ministers of a new covenant, not of the letter but of the Spirit. For the letter kills, but the Spirit gives life" (2 Corinthians 3:4–6).

Cue the tears. Talk about a major moment of conviction. Paul wrote the third chapter of 2 Corinthians to prove his authenticity to the church. He needed them to know that his apostleship was true and that he was the one who brought them the true gospel. But this was not to boast or show off—bragging that he was the greatest apostle of all time. On the contrary! Just as the prophet Moses was carried along by God, so Paul was carried along by God. Think of Moses—an adopted Egyptian turned country boy who was afraid of public speaking. There wasn't much that he could bring to the table for his overwhelming assignment of delivering the Israelites from slavery. But what did God do? He became Moses' sufficiency. And just like Moses, so Paul was testifying to his confidence in Christ. Nothing he did was from his own merit, but from the grace of God.

The message of today's culture is that we are enough on our own. The noise of this movement is deafening, overwhelming individuals of all ages to dig deep within themselves, muster up their own "enoughness," and do it all, because it's weak to rely on anyone other than yourself. But in that moment, after reading Paul's convicting truth, I realized how wrong I had been. I realized how deeply I had fallen into this false message. God had been waiting all along to offer me His sufficiency. His enoughness. His resources. His life. *Himself.*

Oh, what a love—that God would offer us all we need. How mind-blowing that God would equip us and give us everything at His disposal! And why would He do that, you ask? The answer is within 2 Corinthians 3—so that we would become ministers of a new covenant, wholly dependent disciples on a mission to share God's news.

The best gifts are given without any strings attached, and that is exactly what God did for us. Because He created us, He knows us. And because He knows us, He counted the cost and realized we would need a power supply. That we could not be independent apart from Him, but that's okay. This isn't restricting or mean of Him, but truly the most loving act He could ever display.

So it's time we all drop the act. It's time we stop striving for self-sufficiency and independence within ourselves. It's time we stop fighting God's perfect design and just rest in the reality that if He created us, He knows what's best for us. It's time we thank God for making us sufficient—not because of ourselves but because we're connected to Him, covered by Him, and most importantly, saved by Him.

The next time you're tempted to operate out of self-sufficiency, take a moment to pause. Bring yourself back to the beginning. If you're in Christ, remember the gift of God's grace through His salvation to you. Remember your life started in Christ solely based on what He did—not what you did. Not on our works but on God's unmerited favor poured out. When we remember where we truly began with God, we can't help but be dependent on Him. Because we are wholly dependent on God alone for our salvation, we are also wholly dependent on Him for today, tomorrow, and eternity.

Instead of beating yourself up for not being enough, thank God that He makes you enough. Thank God for giving you His sufficiency that promises to work in you and make you more like Him. What a blessing it is to know that God never wants to leave us the same—the more we depend on Him and rely on His sufficiency to sustain us, the more we will become like Him. The more we will be set apart from the world. The more we will taste and see that His plan for our stories is far greater than what we could dream up.

It's time to change our thinking. It's time to let the Holy Spirit reprogram our hearts. Independence apart from God is overrated. Self-sufficiency promises the world but will always let us down. Wholehearted dependence on God is "in," and it's more than a trend. It's the way of God's upside-down kingdom.

Space to Surrender

Such is the confidence that we have through Christ toward God. Not that we are sufficient in ourselves to claim anything as coming from us, but our sufficiency is from God, who has made us sufficient to be ministers of a new covenant, not of the letter but of the Spirit. For the letter kills, but the Spirit gives life.

2 CORINTHIANS 3:4–6

1. Inventory time! Are there any parts of your life where you've been allowing the supposed virtues of independence, hard work, or self-sufficiency cover up your hesitation for living fully surrendered to God?
2. What is your gut reaction to the claim, "We weren't created to be self-sufficient . . . but wholly dependent disciples"? Relieved? Offended? Skeptical? Which do you usually default to—self-sufficiency or dependency?

3. What are some of the biggest "not yets" in your life, where God's timing didn't match up with your hopes and dreams? How did you respond? And for those "not yets" and desires you're facing in your life currently, how can you hand those over to God today?

Lord, thank You for being more than enough. I want to trade in self-sufficiency for freedom found only in You. Help me to take steps day by day to become fully dependent on You.

CHAPTER 4

Trusting God's Timing

Never be afraid to trust an unknown
future to a known God.

CORRIE TEN BOOM

WE'VE ALL HEARD THE STORY before. Maybe you've seen it in your favorite romantic comedy, novel, or even in the life of someone you know. It's a tale as old as time. Girl meets boy, girl falls in love with boy, girl marries boy, and girl starts a family with boy—all in a relatively uncomplicated and quick timeline.

This last weekend, I spent most of my Saturday evening on the couch, watching a few of the Hallmark Channel's Countdown to Christmas movies. I know that there are lots of opinions on

Hallmark movies, but I am not ashamed to say that I am a *big* fan of their Christmas specials. My husband, Michael, always teases me about the franchise, laughing at how painfully predictable each movie is. (He's not wrong, but I still love them, okay?)

A small-town girl moves to the big city to pursue her dreams. Every Christmas she returns to her hometown to visit her family. However, this year is different, because she happens to "randomly" reunite with her old flame slash high school sweetheart. He's either a carpenter, shop owner, swanky business executive, or single dad. Either way, he wears that scruff effortlessly and handsomely. Eventually, after a few awkward encounters, they band together for a cause to save Christmas and—you guessed it—they end up falling in love too. The movie usually ends with a kiss in front of a snowy backdrop, and it's implied that they're headed toward marriage and having kids of their own.

Doesn't that just give you warm and fuzzy feelings? Doesn't that sweet, predictable story just satisfy your sweet, storybook romance itch? Or is that just me?

I think somewhere along the way I, too, adopted that Hallmark storybook idea of love. My childhood consisted of playing dress-up and matchmaker with my Barbies, Polly Pockets (wow, who remembers those?), and friends. It was a rare occasion when the Barbie princess movies, like *Barbie of Swan Lake* and *Barbie in the Nutcracker*, weren't playing on the television in the family room. I dreamed about my wedding and made a list of all the characteristics I wanted in a future husband. And like many of us, I mapped out the perfect scenario and timeline for my love life.

I would not dare thinking about dating anyone until I was out of high school, because I thought that this tender age was too immature. I figured that most high schoolers didn't know what they really wanted at such a young age with puberty and raging hormones. My plan was to focus on my schooling and career and *then*, and only then, find a man I could fall in love with and create our own Hallmark reality. In my mind, it seemed perfect in every way. The blueprint I mapped out had one goal: to whole-heartedly pursue my future, and then, once I had it all together, it would be the right time to add romance into the mix.

But, not surprisingly, God changed the narrative. He rewrote my story. And news flash—it wasn't as picturesque as a Hallmark Christmas hit.

It was sophomore year of high school and I had just broken off a horribly toxic relationship with a boy from my class. Yes, I know what you're thinking. My rigid, well-thought-out plan to wait until after high school to date had already gone out the window. This breakup was especially painful, not because it was true love but because it was my first relationship and it did not start out on the right foot at all.

The word *deceitful* comes to mind when I think of that relationship at sixteen. For the sake of the story, let's call my ex-boyfriend Jake. To be completely transparent, my parents did not like Jake or approve of our desire to be together. They saw red flags that I didn't (don't we just love when our parents are right?) and were concerned that I was getting into a relationship with a nonbeliever. Naively, I believed I could change him. Maybe through my influence he would come to the Lord. But I was the furthest thing from a good influence. This whirlwind romance consisted of lying to my parents when we hung out, deceiving friends and family, and inevitably putting my relationship with God on the back burner.

It may sound dramatic, considering it was all a high school relationship, but breaking up with Jake was painful. I am now happily married with my first baby on the way, and I can't help but let out a sigh of relief. I'm so thankful God got ahold of my stubborn heart and had His way instead of letting me have mine. But in the middle of that breakup, I felt broken—ashamed of my actions and disappointed that I had strayed away from my plan.

The days following the breakup were restorative, albeit uncomfortable. I spent most of my time trying to repair the damage I had caused in the middle of my blind relationship frenzy. I spent each day working to regain my parents' trust after breaking it repeatedly. I spent each day with a remorseful heart, restoring my relationship with God. I spent each day restoring friendships that I had burned and neglected when I was caught up in Jake-world.

The Lord's gentle, merciful, and gracious heart met me in that mess. He met me with an abundance of His love and forgiveness that, with time, healed my shame and guilt. It was a precious time to recommit my life to the Lord—my affections, my priorities, and my purpose. Nearly a year after I had gone off the rails, I remember making this bold declaration to my parents at the dinner table.

"Mom and Dad, I'm going to get back to the basics. I'm going to refocus on my schooling, career, and most importantly, my relationship with God. I've been distracted, but I'm ready to refocus."

After such a train wreck of a relationship, I was ready to kiss dating goodbye. At least for a few years. I was ready to move on and continue following the blueprint I had mapped out for my life. I had gotten off course, but I was determined to get back on, as if I hadn't skipped a beat.

But oh, dear friend. How ironic is our God? How much higher are His ways? Can you guess what happened next?

God's Timing > Mine

It should come as no surprise to you what He did next. Picture this: Tara, now a junior in high school, laser focused. Back on track. Dead set on her goals and willing to bulldoze through any obstacle. She made it a priority to excel in her last years of high school so she could become a doctor. Truly, she wasn't even the slightest bit interested in another relationship. (In fact, she was quite opposed to it after what happened with the last one.)

Now, picture this: Michael, a tall, handsome, and slightly awkward junior who transferred to her high school from out of town.

Can you guess where this is going?

You know, I can't help but smile as I recount this story. Why? Because as I type these words, I am in my office, one door down from Michael's office. That same tall, awkward high school boy is now my husband. This story is so special to me because I can see God's faithfulness and graciousness cover my brokenness. I can see how much more beautiful and perfectly timed His plan was over my own. I can see now, looking back, how deeply and genuinely He can be trusted with our stories.

But I would be lying if I said that I trusted and surrendered to Him fully in the in-between seasons. I would be lying if I said that I didn't struggle with trusting God with my timeline, my expectations, and my unfulfilled longings.

Michael was the gift that I wasn't expecting but, oh my goodness, am I thankful for him. He was the plot twist thrown into the story when I had shut myself off from dating. He was the wild card that completely threw my plans for a loop.

Although I had feelings for this cute boy who stole my heart and made me laugh in AP literature, I was hesitant, to say the least. I finally felt like my parents and I had the restored relationship of trust and friendship that we had before (if not stronger). I finally felt like my relationship with God had started to deepen, and honestly, I was scared to add another distraction into the mix. I finally felt like I had the proper mindset to focus on my pursuit of a medical career and get back to dating *after* I had achieved that. Remember the plan?

But there was something about Michael that gave me indescribable peace. (I'm sorry this isn't a book about "how to know if he's the one" or "how to know if you're ready to date." Maybe another time.) Before we became "official" and started dating, Michael and I spent a lot of time with our families. Think of it as our family chaperoning our dates. I told Michael what I had been through in the last year, and we both agreed that we needed to take it slow. Eventually, after a few months of spending time together, getting to know each other and our families (along with much prayer), we officially started dating.

On a typical day you would find us going to school and spending time together once all our homework and sports were finished for the day. Some of our favorite ways to spend quality time together were trying new restaurants, hitting up the theater for a movie, hanging out with our families, and binge watching our favorite show, *Psych*. Two high school sweethearts, blissfully entangled in the beginning stages of a romantic relationship.

Yet as the time went by, the Hallmark fantasy filter began to soften. I'm not saying that our relationship went downhill. On the contrary, Michael and I are truly blessed to have such a steady love story. But the road that was once easy and stress-free began to fade in the distance.

Suddenly, impatience was the houseguest that would not take the hint and leave. It set up residence in my mind and relentlessly pummeled me with questions like, "Why aren't you married yet? Why hasn't Michael proposed? When is that next step going to come?"

Over time, those questions brought me to this conclusion: God's timing wasn't good enough. God's plan was taking too long.

Is God's Timing Really Perfect?

When our two-year dating anniversary rolled around, something clicked inside of me. I became completely and utterly obsessed with getting engaged. I started feeling increasingly angry with God and distrustful of His supposed perfect timing. Almost every week, like clockwork, I would crawl to my mom in tears. It was the same sob story. I complained about God's ridiculously slow timing, and she would listen patiently. I threw myself a pity party, lamenting over the fact that God was torturing me by making me wait so long for an engagement ring.

Looking back years later, I can see exactly what was going on. My old struggle with the myth of control was back for another round—rearing its ugly head, shovel-feeding me the lie that my timing and my ideas were better than God's.

After each of our conversations, my mother would lovingly hand me a tissue, embrace me, and say something along the lines of, "Trust God's timing."

Boy, did I *hate* when she said that. Every time without fail, that phrase made my skin crawl, as if nails were screeching down a chalkboard. The reality is that I didn't see the appeal of trusting God and His timing. Like, what was the big whoop? Did it really make a difference to trust God? If I was being honest, during my younger years when I was going to church, reading the Bible, and doing the "good Christian girl" things, it had all felt more like empty words than anything. It all sounded nice, but I'd never really believed it, nor did I care to have my life changed by it. When push came to shove, I didn't want to trust God if He wasn't going to move things along fast enough for my liking.

Instead of seeking to understand what trusting God truly meant, I nodded politely in agreement when someone would say to trust Him. I tried to hide an annoyed expression when a loved one or pastor would encourage me to trust God with all my heart.

But all of that changed when I was backed into a corner—when God left me no other option than to fully rely on Him. And I am so thankful He did.

If you're anything like me, this idea of trusting God sounds nice, but you have no idea where to start. Perhaps you've been told to trust God your whole life, but you've never really known why. I'm here to tell you that you're not alone, and there are answers just around the corner. But before continuing my story, let's dig into some biblical background.

The Theology of Trust

In ancient Bible times, the same Hebrew word was used to describe both the act of trusting God and the art of welding. Those may sound like the two most unrelated ideas in the entire world; stick with me.

This word is *batach*. It originally referred to the the fusing of two pieces to make one solid object. Indulge me for a moment and let's do a deep dive into the process of welding. The first step in welding begins with an artisan taking multiple pieces of metal with an end goal in mind—to create a tool, weapon, or piece of equipment. Next, the welder throws the pieces into a scorching fire. (A quick Google search informed me that the fire needs to be anywhere from 3,000 to 10,000 degrees Fahrenheit. Yikes.) The reason for subjecting the pieces to such a blistering fire is to soften them and ensure they are moldable, flexible, and workable. Once the pieces reach the desired temperature, the welder joins them all together and uses his hammer to forge them. The combination of heat, time, and pressure must all work together for this project to be a success. At the end of this tedious process, the welder has created for himself a beautiful tool. The many different pieces of metal have not only become solid and sturdy but completely inseparable.

Whoever decided to relate the act of trusting God to the art of welding was onto something. Think about it this way: Trust connects us to our heavenly Father. It binds us into an interwoven relationship with Him. Think of trust as a process that welds us to God and makes us a part of Him through deep dependence.

So back to my story of learning to trust God's timing. I'd finally reached a point where I wanted to know what it meant to truly trust God because, frankly, nothing else I had tried was working. After crying my eyes out to my mom for the hundredth time, I realized that something needed to change. But there was a ginormous, overwhelming wall to overcome in front of me: I had zero clue what to do. I had no idea how to practically live that out. My feeble attempts to control the timing of my life always left me empty and wanting more. Every time I trusted in my own abilities to control the outcome, it was as if I had taken two steps forward and sixteen steps back. None of that frustration helped me know how to start trusting God, and I mean *really* trusting Him in the middle of my pain and frustration. Maybe you can relate.

As the rest of this chapter unfolds, I invite you to go on an expedition with me. Ready your heart with me as we zoom in closer and uncover this idea of trust—which, spoiler alert, isn't actually as overwhelming as it may seem. We're here to find God's answers to the questions we have, such as: *What does trusting God really mean?* and *How can God really be trusted when my plans are falling apart?*

TRUST IS THE KEY THAT UNLOCKS GENUINE, OPENHANDED SURRENDER TO GOD.

My hope is that you'll walk away from this chapter knowing that truly trusting God goes hand in hand with releasing our control and surrendering to Him. We can't have one without the other. We can't enjoy the freedom and peace that comes from surrender without simultaneously learning to trust in God's goodness and timing. Without putting our trust in the proper place—in Christ—every act of surrender will be followed by another attempt to retake control, and we will remain stuck in that cycle until we learn to trust.

Trust is the key that unlocks genuine, openhanded surrender to God.

When All Else Fails, God Doesn't

One of my favorite Bible characters is Abraham, the father of many nations. Do you remember that Sunday school song? "Father Abraham had many sons, and many sons had Father Abraham . . ." (I apologize in advance for how that tune may be stuck in your head for days. It's stuck in my head now too!)

As I've gotten older, I've realized there are a lot of ways I can relate to Abraham. We usually consider Abraham as one of God's favorites, one whom He chose to create an everlasting covenant with. Although that's true, there's so much more to Abraham and his story. If we're being super honest, Abraham was a doubtful, distrusting, and sneaky guy. He may have been someone God chose to make a covenant with, and he showed tremendous faith when he uprooted his entire family and chose to follow God into the wilderness—but he still struggled day in and day out to live according to his faith.

One of Abraham's greatest struggles was believing God to be trustworthy—believing that His word and His timing would come to pass. Instead of trusting God to do what He said, Abraham's actions reflected a need for personal control—a desire to plan and manipulate instead of surrender. Here's the scene: God told Abraham, "Look up at the sky and count the stars—if indeed you can count them. . . . So shall your offspring be" (Genesis 15:5 NIV). I can only imagine the reaction of Abraham and his wife, Sarah, to this news, considering that they were, frankly, old as dirt. Sarah was *way* past childbearing age. And yet God asked them to trust Him and His promises.

You would think that after receiving this promise from God himself, Abraham and Sarah would just sit back and trust. Wait. Persevere with patience. Have faith. But that's never how these stories seem to go, am I right? In Genesis 16 we read a story that's very strange and a bit shocking to our modern sensibilities. Abraham and Sarah decided to take matters into their own hands. Instead of trusting God's methods and timing, Sarah persuaded Abraham to conceive a child with her Egyptian maidservant. In that moment Sarah decided to snatch the steering wheel away from the Lord and steer their life's course in a different direction. If their offspring were going to be as numerous as the stars, then why hadn't God given her children yet? It was time to take over.

Abraham listened to his wife. And Hagar, the maidservant, gave birth to a child. Even though this had been Sarah's plan, do you think she was happy that she got her way?

Nope.

Abraham and Sarah's joint decision to take personal control over their lives didn't result in sunshine and rainbows like they thought. It resulted in marital tension, the exile of poor, innocent Hagar and her son, and failure to trust God's promises.

But there's a silver lining to this strange and disappointing story. There's some good news. God *still* kept His promise. God *still* kept His word and used Abraham, despite his lack of trust, to be the father of many nations. None of this came as a surprise to God. The fact that Abraham and Sarah operated out of self-sufficiency and took their chance at personal control did not deter God from being faithful to His promises.

That's how powerful and sovereign God's promises and plans are. They prevail even when His children try to grasp for control.

What God Can Do with Our Trust

There's a verse I love, although it's super hard for me to hear sometimes. Each time a holiday, anniversary, or special occasion would come and pass with no engagement ring, the Lord would convict my heart with this verse. Each time I put God on blast for supposedly not caring about my life or having good plans for me, He would drop this truth bomb on my heart: "Trust in the LORD with all your heart, and do not lean on your own understanding.

In all your ways acknowledge him, and he will make straight your paths" (Proverbs 3:5–6).

Do you remember the dilemma in the garden? Do you remember when we talked about the origin of this whole issue of control in the first chapter? It all began in Eden. It all began with Adam and Eve and humanity leaning on their own understanding.

Jon Bloom, teacher and cofounder of Desiring God, wrote this: "If you eat of that one tree, you will be saying to me [God], 'I'm smarter than you. I am more authoritative than you. I am wiser than you. I think I can care for myself better than you care for me. You are not a very good Father. And so, I am going to reject you.'"[3]

Isn't that what this is all about? Leaning on our own understanding and trusting ourselves instead of God lead us back to the myth of control. They lead us to this false sense of self-sufficiency—that we are enough on our own and we know better than God. Bloom calls this the "insanity of trusting ourselves."[4]

On the flip side you and I have been given the gift of *sanity* through the Lord—the joyful gift of trusting the Lord instead of leaning on our own understanding. When nothing makes sense to the world, God gives us the ability to stay sane and grounded in Him. (That's another one of those upside-down–kingdom truths.)

You see, God hasn't left us to our own devices. He hasn't left us to figure it out as we go, within our own selves. Instead, He lovingly offers us to daily *batach*—to weld ourselves to Him. To choose each day to be, oh, so connected to His heart, His will, and His Word.

If you were to ask me if I was trusting God and His timing above my own, I would have most likely told you yes. But there was obviously a part of me that was not acknowledging Him as the One who was directing my every step. It's one thing to say or think that God is trustworthy, but it's another thing to actually believe it and live according to it. When King Solomon wrote, "In all your ways acknowledge him," in Proverbs 3:6, he wasn't merely telling us to notice God in all things. He wasn't saying to casually glance over at Him with a nonchalant, "Oh, hi, I didn't see You there."

The Hebrew word *yada* (translated in Proverbs 3 as *acknowledge*) means "to know." Solomon is telling us to be deeply acquainted with God, to know with certainty who God is.

This is more than noticing God. It's about *knowing God*.

That, right there, is the difference. If we don't know who the Lord is and if we don't know what He's promised us in His Word, then how can we trust Him? (We're going to talk about this more in chapter 8, so stay tuned.) Acknowledging God means being intimately connected to Him. And how do we stay in that intimate connection? By welding ourselves to Him through the beautiful gift that is trust.

When God Gives You a Red Light

I know all of this is easier said than done. Trust me—I've been preaching this message for the last few years of my life and still struggle to trust God, especially in the hard times. And I think that's something important we need to recognize. It's easier to say we trust God when things are going our way. When we have our dream job. When we're dating the perfect guy. But when our plans don't pan out the way we expected and when we're backed into a corner, trusting God seems like the hardest thing to do.

I have a theory on that if you'll indulge me. I wonder if trusting God is so hard at times because we're afraid that if we trust

Him, He will mess with our plans. I remember thinking that if I trusted God's timing for my engagement, I wouldn't get what I wanted. That if I trusted Him, it meant I had to follow what He had for me—and that wouldn't be as ideal as what I had planned. And that just wasn't going to fly. It sounds ridiculous to say it out loud, but I suspected that if I trusted God and acknowledged Him in all my ways, I wouldn't get engaged as soon as I wanted. Wow, that may be one of the most vulnerable things I've ever said, friend, but we're here to lay it all out on the line.

As fickle human beings, we naturally do not want to hear God tell us, *Hey, you're making plans, but I'm going to change them.* For some people, that may be encouraging—the fact that God disrupts our plans. But for most of us, if we're being honest, we absolutely hate hearing that. What I struggled to understand was why God would ask me to trust Him and wait so long when my desire for engagement was a *good* desire. It was a *good* plan for a *good* thing. God created marriage and loves marriage, right? So why wouldn't He affirm me in my timing? Why wouldn't He let me get to that good season of life sooner?

Maybe you can think of a good plan and good desire that you have right now. Maybe it's something like mine—getting engaged and starting a family. Maybe it's being involved in a certain church ministry. Maybe it's getting a job so you can be a good steward of your talents and abilities and provide for yourself and your family. Friend, there are a lot of *good* desires—blessings to enjoy and work to do that furthers the kingdom of God. There's nothing wrong with those good desires. But for some reason, God may be asking you to wait. He may even want you to go in a different direction—away from those good things. This doesn't mean our desires and dreams are invalid. This doesn't mean we should stop dreaming altogether.

This just means we need to set our dreams and desires for our lives at the feet of Jesus, trusting that He knows what we desire, but more importantly that He wants to give us what is best. Even if His best is not what we were expecting.

So what do you do when you're stopped at a red light instead of given the green light to go?

My conversations with God used to go a lot like this: "Lord, what the heck! I'm not asking You for a million dollars. I'm not asking You to help me rob a bank or something bad like that. I'm asking You for marriage. Something that's good, right? What's the deal?"

Do you remember the story of King David in 2 Samuel 7? David had a brilliant idea to build God a temple. He wanted to show God how much he loved Him by building a beautiful dwelling place designed to honor Him for all He had done for His people. Seems like a nice idea, right?

But God answered in the most surprising way. He told David no. Not right now. Hold up. He told him to wait and trust. He told him to put a halt on his plans, however well intended they were. Instead of complaining to the Lord, what did David do? He listened. He received the word of God. He saw God's no as the beginning of the conversation and the beginning of his story—not the end. Because he had practiced welding himself to the Lord in trust throughout his life, David didn't see God's no as a reason to distrust Him, but as a reason to persevere, knowing that God had something better planned. And eventually, in His perfect timing, in accordance with His perfect plan, God gave the green light.

I recently found out my husband hadn't seen one of my favorite movies, *Hacksaw Ridge*, starring Andrew Garfield. I knew we had to watch it. If you've seen the movie, you know it's based on the true story of Desmond Doss, a combat medic in World War II. Although he was a Seventh-day Adventist pacifist, Desmond wanted nothing more than to serve in the military. Although he had a conviction from the Lord not to kill, even in war, he wanted to be a soldier.

Like all of us, Desmond started planning. Once accepted into the military, he told God, "I'm going to be a soldier in Your army." God said, "No, Desmond. You're going to be a field medic." That wasn't necessarily the outcome Desmond had in mind. That was a prime example of God destroying his plans.

And yet, at the end of Desmond's life, he had racked up an astonishing number of medals. He was awarded the Bronze Star and the Medal of Honor for saving seventy-five men in the Battle of Okinawa. All as a field medic and all without killing. All because he made plans but listened when the Lord said no. All because, although it was a rocky journey, Desmond chose to trust that God had a better story for him than he could have planned for himself.

Oswald Chambers, a twentieth-century pastor and author, wanted nothing more in life than to launch a seminary school for pastors. That was his plan from the beginning. He and his wife bought a building and were so excited to begin. Then World War I started, and they had to close their building. In the middle of his broken dreams and plans, he asked God what to do. And God sent Oswald and his wife to Egypt, of all places. They lived in a tent in the desert, preaching to soldiers. Not exactly what he had planned or even wanted.

But do you want to know one of many amazing things that God did with Oswald's trust? Mrs. Chambers never left her husband's side, taking copious and detailed notes of his teachings. After Oswald died she took her journal to a publishing house, and those very same words fill the pages of *My Utmost for His Highest*, one of the most influential books of the Christian faith.

Sweet friend, sometimes our dreams and the things we want out of life aren't bad, but God has a bigger plan that He wants us to acknowledge. He wants our trust more than He wants our plans. He wants our surrender and dependence rather than our blueprint. He wants us to taste and see that if we only trust Him, He has immeasurably more in store than we could ever ask or imagine (Ephesians 3:20–21).

You see, when we choose to trust God and loosen our clenched fists, it frees up our hearts to sense the beauty of His plans and purposes. It clears our tunnel vision that only focuses on what we want and opens our eyes to the surpassing potential in Christ.

How to Practically Build Our Trust in the Lord

So what does this all mean? How can we take the concept of trusting God and put it into action in our hearts, minds, and lives? As we talked about earlier, it's one thing to say we trust God with our stories, and it's another to actually live out that trust moment by moment and day by day. But it turns out there are a lot of ways we can build our trust in the Lord. In fact, God's Word provides some concrete guidance for us to follow—and you can start right now, no matter where you find yourself.

- **Actively cast your cares on God.** The apostle Peter says in 1 Peter 5:7 to "cast all your anxiety on him because he cares for you" (NIV). In this chapter Peter emphasizes the necessity of humbling ourselves before God, lowering ourselves and recognizing our need for the Lord's help. To cast our cares means to *throw off* or *hurl* our anxieties upon God. So casting our cares on God demonstrates that we trust Him. When we acknowledge our worries but choose to surrender and commit them to God, it shows we trust His ability to do what only He can do.

- **Immerse yourself deeply in God's Word each day.** One of the most life-changing practices that has helped me go from distrusting to trusting the Lord is spending quality time with Him in the Bible each day. The more we read His promises, recount His faithfulness, and get to know His heart through time spent in Scripture, the more we will trust Him. It's not only a command and desire from our heavenly Father to read His Word, but a blessing and opportunity to thrive in our faith, build our trust, and fall in love with the dependable God we serve.

- **Demonstrate patience and perseverance in your relationship with God.** Oof, if I had a nickel for how many times in my life God made me wait, I would be a bazillionaire. Impatience made me feel God was just sitting back, not working or caring about my life. Impatience made me believe that God wasn't good because His plans were not mine. But here's the catch: a heart that waits patiently for the Lord is a heart that welds itself to God. Waiting is a beautiful picture of deep trust in God, a willingness to stick it out with Him, no matter the cost, no matter the timing, because He's sovereign. Isaiah 40 is a chapter about God's

> WAITING IS A BEAUTIFUL PICTURE OF DEEP TRUST IN GOD.

71

sovereignty and power over everything. The good times and bad. The hard and the good. Although we may grow tired and weak, God will renew us and strengthen us if we wait on Him. If we trust in Him. If we stay connected to Him.

One of my favorite pastors, Ben Stuart, says it this way: "When we know God's plan, we can rest."[5] When we trust that God is enough and His plans are immeasurably more than we could have planned or orchestrated, we can stop striving. We can cease the endless cycle of feeling frustrated or disappointed with the outcome of our lives because we have a God who is more than enough. Who never leaves His children wanting but always satisfies them with good things.

If we want to be people who live a life of surrender, we must embark on the beautiful journey that is trusting God. And because we serve a truly good God, when we're faced with the choice of clenching our fists or trusting God, we will never regret choosing trust.

Space to Surrender

Trust in the LORD with all your heart,
    and do not lean on your own understanding.
In all your ways acknowledge him,
    and he will make straight your paths.

PROVERBS 3:5–6

1. Do you have a problem with trust—whether trusting other people or trusting God? Why or why not?
2. What's your typical reaction when God's plan is different than yours?
3. In all honesty and vulnerability, what is one plan, dream, or goal you have that you are afraid God might turn upside down?
4. What is one way you can practice trusting God? Feel free to borrow from the three strategies I gave in this chapter: casting your cares, immersing yourself in the Word, and demonstrating patience and perseverance with God.

Lord, when I try to hold on to control, it's a recipe for disappointment and exhaustion. Help me to trust You. I want nothing more than the peace that comes from resting in You and trusting Your timing.

CHAPTER 5

A Holy Power Source

The Holy Spirit never enters a man and lets him
live like the world. You can be sure of that.

A. W. TOZER

THE PROCESS OF WRITING THIS book has taught me so many things about myself. I've learned that my best writing is done in silence. I've learned that a Yeti water bottle filled to the brim with a few lemon slices and a flickering candle are essential. I've also learned to give myself grace and tons of opportunities to nap during the writing process. Man, is it sanctifying. And I've accepted the fact that I need a break every few hours to scour the snack cupboard. (Dove dark chocolate squares have been my book-writing fuel, let me tell you.)

But the most important lesson I've learned along the way is this: I have not perfected the art of surrendering. When it comes to releasing control, surrendering my life, and trusting God instead, I have not fully "arrived." This shouldn't come as a shock to you, but none of this comes easy. Even though the Lord has grown and refined me more than I could have ever imagined in these areas, I *still* struggle. Every day, I wake up and battle against the urge to clench my fists, take hold of the steering wheel, and choose personal control.

My pink-colored Instagram feed and filtered stories could potentially give the illusion that my life is "perfect." I may be sharing devotionals, podcast episodes, and other lessons about the Christian life, but I still struggle. The reality is I'm just a twenty-three-year-old girl who lives in the same small town she grew up in. I don't have an advanced degree. If you were to walk into my house, 99 percent of the time, you would find me wearing sweatpants, a baggy crewneck, and my cushy house slippers. Oh, and no makeup. Let's be real.

In other words, I'm a pretty average, run-of-the-mill human being. And although sometimes social media may not convey it, I fight some messy battles against control on a daily basis. I want to set the record straight, so let me reintroduce myself.

Hi. My name is Tara. I'm a recovering control freak.

I don't want you to forget that we're all in this together. I'm running this race called life with you. And most importantly, God certainly hasn't left us without help.

When it comes to surrendering our lives to the Lord, the hard truth is we can't expect it to happen naturally or instantaneously.

And we most certainly can't expect our old flesh, our sinful nature, not to rear its ugly head every now and again to try to convince us that control is better. As we learned in the last few chapters, trusting God and surrendering is not a passive lifestyle. It's an active pursuit.

That may sound like an Instagram-ready quote—"An active pursuit, not a passive lifestyle"—but if we're being completely honest, it also sounds exhausting, doesn't it? You might be wondering how in the world we are supposed to release our death grip on control and trust God instead of ourselves. After all, we're only human.

I hear you and I feel you. And that is why I'm so excited about this chapter. Friend, I want tell you some really—and I mean really—good news.

We don't have to do it on our own.

Take a deep breath. Release the tension in your shoulders. Shake off the pressure to perform. We don't have to fumble our way around in the dark, trying to put all the puzzle pieces together on our own. On the contrary, everything we need—and more—is right here. Right in front of us. Right at our fingertips.

Let me introduce you, or reintroduce you, to someone called the Holy Spirit.

Clearing the Fog

My first children's Bible introduced me to the Holy Trinity. I remember flipping through the chunky board book Bible as a young child and slowly learning about the Father, Son, and Holy Spirit. It's a ridiculously deep concept even for adults—the idea that one God could be three persons—so you can imagine a young child had some trouble grasping the idea of the triune God.

As I grew older, Sunday school lessons, sermons, and Bible studies helped me understand a lot about the first two persons of the Trinity: the Father and the Son. But there was always a big question mark that hung over the third person, the Holy Spirit. He's the divine person I never really sought to learn more about because, frankly, He seemed *too* spiritual for my tiny mind to fathom. I just didn't bother to dig deeper.

I suspect I'm not alone in this. Maybe you're right there with me. We see God the Creator of the universe, our covenant keeper, the Great I Am, our loving Father. We see Jesus clearly—Son of God, Savior of humankind, sent to ransom us from death. But the picture starts to blur with this Holy Spirit figure. The other names to describe him (like the Paraclete) don't necessarily help us gain clarity. And the Holy Ghost sounds a little spooky, doesn't it? Almost *Ghostbuster*-y?

Whether you've grown up in the church hearing about this Holy Spirit character your whole life, or you're new to the faith and have zero clue who He is, or you're somewhere in the middle, this chapter is for you. You see, the Holy Spirit is essential to living a life of surrender.

We can't do it without Him, but thank God we don't have to.

An Encounter with the Holy Spirit

Never in my entire life did I think I would want to be in any sort of ministry. From a young age, everyone said my brother, Lee, would make a great pastor. They were drawn to his exuberant personality and his contagious joy that flowed from the Lord. I was perfectly content with *not* receiving those praises, because, as we've talked about, I was on the fast track to medical school. As far as I was concerned, my church and ministerial involvement would probably look like volunteering in the nursery, serving here and there, and showing up to church each Sunday.

A lot of my peers planned to go to a Christian university after high school with dreams of graduating seminary or focusing on some sort of biblical studies degree. That was fine and dandy for them, but I had no desire to be trained in ministry. Zero. Zilch. Nada. Again—that wasn't part of the plan.

But after dropping out of college, for the first time in my life I was starting to think about ministry. There was something nudging me, a funny feeling in the pit of my stomach that wouldn't leave me alone. And God began to open surprising doors that seemed to be marked "ministry."

One cold, winter day, a mentor of mine from my church took me out to coffee. "Fill me in on your life," I remember her starting. It was a simple question, but it opened up the floodgates. I began telling her how stuck I felt after God called me home from Oregon State University. How disappointed I was that none of my plans seemed to be working out and how anxious I was to jump into the next thing. But I didn't dare say that something inside of me was screaming *ministry*. I didn't dare admit that I was even considering it. At that point it was still a new, fleeting thought. It was a rumbling inside of me that I still wasn't convinced was anything more than indigestion and nerves.

After I had bared my soul and exposed my painfully vulnerable emotions, my mentor asked, "Have you ever thought about pursuing ministry or Bible school?"

She must have noticed my jaw on the floor. Not even my boyfriend or parents knew about this inkling deep within my soul yet. It was a feeling so far out in left field that I had been afraid to vocalize it or even entertain it. I didn't think I was the ideal candidate for any type of ministry or Bible schooling: a college dropout, an ex-retail employee, and an unreliable chronic illness warrior.

"I don't know, Tara. I just have this sense from the Holy Spirit," my mentor said with a shrug.

A Holy Power Source

If you had just a few more days to live, what would you say to your closest family and friends?

This is a question I often ask myself. Sometimes I brainstorm what crazy deep words of wisdom or groundbreaking encouragement I would give. How would I leave my loved ones with a big mic-drop moment before I died?

In Jesus' final days on earth, He took full advantage of the time He had left just to be with His disciples. Serve them. Love on them. Pray for them. Speak over them. Break bread with them.

Jesus could have said anything, and I mean *anything*, before ascending to heaven. He could have told them details about the growth of the church over the next hundred years, and how they would flourish and prevail despite the persecution they would face. He could have spoken to each disciple individually, foretelling exactly what the rest of their lives would look like. But instead of sharing that kind of information, He left them with a gift.

After washing His disciples' feet and foreshadowing His impending betrayal by Judas, Jesus comforted His disciples. He spoke encouragement into their lives, rallying them to continue believing and persevering in the faith. At the end of his mini sermon, Jesus promised the ultimate form of comfort. The ultimate gift.

> These things I have spoken to you while I am still with you. But the Helper, the Holy Spirit, whom the Father will send in my name, he will teach you all things and bring to your remembrance all that I have said to you. Peace I leave with you; my peace I give to you. Not as the world gives do I give to you. Let not your hearts be troubled, neither let them be afraid. You heard me say to you, "I am going away, and I will come to you." (John 14:25–28)

On the surface this was probably not the most reassuring sentiment—their Savior and best friend telling them He was going to leave. Right? But in typical Jesus fashion, even though He was leaving, He still had a plan for providing the disciples with all the comfort and help they would need to live.

Help Is on the Way

I remember the Spirit feeling kind of fuzzy and being described in an ambiguous way in the Old Testament. And that was even when He was mentioned, which is only occasionally. Perhaps you've noticed Him in your reading of certain books like Exodus or Zechariah. I wonder if the disciples felt the same way. They probably did, because God used His Son, Jesus, to make the picture crystal clear in the New Testament.

In just a matter of days after Jesus' conversation with the disciples that night, He would hang on a cross, be buried in a tomb, rise from the dead, and then depart from earth to rejoin His Father in heaven. He was gearing up for His final act. But even though Jesus was leaving, He also planned to stay via the Holy Spirit.

Now let's use some logic here. Unlike the twelve disciples, we modern-day believers do not have the physical presence of Jesus among us. As much as we wish we did, as much as we wish we could sit across from Jesus at our favorite coffee shop and chat, that's just not our reality. But what we do have is the Holy Spirit, whom Jesus sent to be our helper and guide. Here and now. Living and active.

So if all of that is true, then we cannot neglect the Holy Spirit. If all of that is true, then we desperately need Him and His empowerment to live the life that God has called us to. If all of that is true, then we don't have to strive and try to release control, surrender, and trust God on our own. The truth of the matter, as we've learned, is we can't live surrendered to God through our own strength. It's too easy to slip back into our old ways of bearing down on control and not wanting to let up. But the good news is we have a helper who makes surrendering our lives and trusting God not only possible but beautifully worth it.

Our power source, the One who supplies us with everything we need for life and godliness, the reason we can be victorious over the myth of control, is the Holy Spirit Himself, present and available to all believers.

Who the Holy Spirit Is and Is Not

Sometimes the easiest way to understand something is to first acknowledge what it is *not*. For instance, we know that love is *not* hate. We know that love is *not* arrogant or rude (1 Corinthians 13:4). Starting with a clear baseline of what love is not helps us understand what love truly is.

The same can be helpful in our study of the Holy Spirit. Let's break it down.

The Holy Spirit is *not*

- a ghost that flies around with a white sheet on its head,
- a fictional character,
- a secondary person of the Trinity whom we shouldn't bother knowing,
- another name for our own feelings, or
- a puppet that we can manipulate to fit our agendas.

But the Holy Spirit *is*

- a unique person who is fully and completely divine just like the Father and the Son,
- the Christian's helper and teacher, and
- the Christian's power source and enablement.

THE HOLY SPIRIT AS A PERSON

Have you ever heard the Spirit described as an *it*? That's pretty common, but I think it's important to remember that He's a person. When we say *He* instead of *it*, we remind ourselves of the reality that the Holy Spirit is not just an energy field, some kind of impersonal force, or a random voice in our head—He's a person who is active, present, and powerful in our lives.

This isn't the place for a complete theological meditation on the doctrine of the Trinity—though there are some great books out there on exactly that topic, and I totally recommend studying up on our beautiful, mysterious, three-in-one God. The aim of this chapter is simply to open the eyes of our hearts and rewire our brains to recognize the Holy Spirit as a personal counselor without whom it would be impossible to live a surrendered life.

THE HOLY SPIRIT AS A HELPER

When I was about eight years old, I started volunteering in the nursery at church on Sunday mornings. That hour mainly consisted of holding sleepy babies, consoling others who were upset, and chasing the more active ones around. The older women who volunteered in the nursery called me their little helper.

The word *helper* is important in the Bible. In Genesis God told Adam that it wasn't good for him to be alone, and He provided Adam with a helper, Eve. Adam recognized Eve as "bone of my bones and flesh of my flesh" (2:23), revealing their close, personal connection. The two of them together were created in God's image and called to partner together in living out God's plan for humanity.

The Greek word for *helper* in the New Testament is *parakletos*, which is why we sometimes call the Holy Spirit the Paraclete. *Parakletos* can mean "advocate," such as when someone pleads another's case in a court of law. We see that meaning in 1 John 2:1, where the word is actually used to describe Jesus' advocating for sinners with the Father.

Usually, *parakletos* is used to describe the Holy Spirit as our helper—one who comes alongside to exhort, encourage, and lighten. Jesus didn't merely say the Holy Spirit would be an infrequent babysitter (like me in the church nursery), but a *constant* aid and encourager to every believer.

The Holy Spirit's work as our helper covers a lot more

territory than many of us realize. The Holy Spirit isn't just help-ful in character, He *is* help. He personifies and embodies help. He is constantly with us, as Jesus promised. In fact, Matthew 28:20 guarantees the Spirit's constant presence in our lives: "And surely I am with you always, to the very end of the age" (NIV).

What would it look like if we really embraced the truth that the Holy Spirit is an ever-present gift, that He is always at our disposal, ready to help with absolutely everything? The big details and the small details? The mundane, day-to-day decisions as well as the life-altering decisions? I like to think of the Holy Spirit sit-ting right next to me—here at my side as I write, in the passenger seat of my car, in the grocery store pushing my cart with me, and every other place my two feet are planted each day.

One thing I've learned on my journey toward surrender is to always take help when it's offered. Do you remember chap-ter 3? We talked about how independence is overrated—how the Christian life was designed to operate out of dependence and not self-sufficiency. When we refuse to see the Holy Spirit's role as our helper as a good gift, it's usually because we are believing the lie that we can do it on our own. The lie that needing help is somehow a flaw or that relying on someone else to come to our aid and rescue is the easy way out.

But Jesus' upside-down kingdom reminds us that we were created for help. We weren't created to operate out of ourselves. Jesus knew that His people would need someone greater than themselves after He left to rejoin His Father in heaven. He fore-saw that we would need constant help and guidance. Whether you're thinking of daily faithfulness or the church's mission to share the good news of Jesus, the journey is going to be chock-full of really hard decisions and circumstances. But praise be to God

> BECAUSE OF JESUS' GUARANTEED GIFT OF THE SPIRIT, WE'RE FULLY EQUIPPED FOR EVERYTHING LIFE MAY THROW AS US.

that He loves us enough not to leave us alone. Because of Jesus' guaranteed gift of the Spirit, we're fully equipped for everything life may throw at us. In the apostle Peter's words, "His divine power has granted to us all things that pertain to life and godliness, through the knowledge of him who called us to his own glory and excellence" (2 Peter 1:3).

THE HOLY SPIRIT AS OUR POWER SOURCE

Every year, without fail, my parents signed my brother and me up for Awana Clubs, a weekly youth group of sorts for kids in elementary school. On a typical night we would sing songs, play games, and work through our Scripture memory books. The goal was to memorize as many verses as possible to complete your book and earn your badges. Well, the main goal was to hide God's Word in our hearts, but the iron-on badges and tokens to cash out for prizes were a plus.

Out of the hundreds of verses I learned during my time in Awana, Romans 8:9 has stuck with me—but if I'm being completely transparent, the reason it stuck with me was that I found it utterly confusing: "You, however, are not in the flesh but in the Spirit, if in fact the Spirit of God dwells in you. Anyone who does not have the Spirit of Christ does not belong to him."

What in the world was the apostle Paul trying to communicate when he wrote this verse? *I don't know about you, Paul, but I definitely have flesh on my body,* eight-year-old Tara would think to herself with a furrowed brow. But I eventually learned I was missing the point. When someone gives their life to Christ, they become a child of God—they belong to God. When Paul wrote that those who belong to God are not "in the flesh," he simply meant we are no longer defined by our earthly, bodily life and sin nature. Our sins have been forgiven, death is no longer the end, and the hope of heaven changes everything about the way we live here and now. Paul told us that Christians do not belong in the flesh anymore *because* the Spirit indwells them. Because the Spirit comes upon every believer, they are not to operate or live out of their old flesh any longer.

I used to think of the Holy Spirit as an add-on. If you've ever been to the burger joint Five Guys, you're probably familiar with their big selling point: how easy it is to customize your burger. Perhaps you're just a straight up, plain cheeseburger fan. But why stop there? Five Guys lets you add on bacon, lettuce, A.1. Sauce . . . whatever you want, they offer. That's honestly how I viewed the Holy Spirit—an add-on to my spiritual life. Not an essential part of my life but a nice thing to throw on when I felt like it or when I wanted to look or sound holy.

But Romans 8:9 doesn't tell us that the Spirit merely adds on to our lives. God's Word says the Spirit *dwells* in us. In the Old Testament, the word *dwell* was used to paint a metaphorical, mental picture of God pitching a tent and living among and abiding with His people. The fact that the Spirit dwells in every believer refers to an intimate connection, a permanent residence. Not an add-on to your burger for fifty cents. An intimate relationship.

Think about your curling iron, toaster, or really anything that has a long cord and plug. Without taking the two prongs and plugging them into an outlet, you can't achieve that beautiful curl, and your toast won't turn a lovely, golden color. Why? Because it's

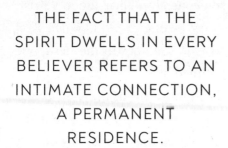

THE FACT THAT THE SPIRIT DWELLS IN EVERY BELIEVER REFERS TO AN INTIMATE CONNECTION, A PERMANENT RESIDENCE.

not connected to a power source. Because that tool is specifically designed to run off electrical power. Nowadays, countless tools are wireless—our phones, your favorite Bluetooth speaker, the handheld vacuum. But even wireless power tools need to be plugged into a power source to maintain a charge and function properly.

The same goes for you and me. The Holy Spirit is like an electrical circuit, and without relying on and acknowledging the Holy Spirit's power in our lives, we will not be able to live according to our new flesh, as Paul wrote in Romans 8. The Spirit is not only our helper, guide, advocate, and teacher, but He's also our conduit, or connector, to the heart and truth of our heavenly Father.

With the Holy Spirit, Surrender Is Possible

Only a matter of months after that coffee date with my mentor, I decided to enroll online in Bible college. And it was only a matter of months after that coffee date that I decided to sign up for a free WordPress blog site, open an Instagram account, and start telling people about my testimony and my Jesus, sharing what God was teaching me in this new season.

The funny thing about letting the Holy Spirit have His way in your life is that 99.9 percent of the time, it doesn't make sense to you. It usually surprises you or flips what you thought on its head. It usually calls you out into uncomfortable places.

That was certainly how I felt when I finally stopped trying to redesign my life's blueprint. Even being open to ministry, not to mention taking the first step by enrolling in Bible school, represented a major step toward surrender, and it wasn't at all clear to me how it fit with my past or what it would mean for my future. But the joy in allowing the Holy Spirit to be your guide, your counselor, and your power source is that He always leads you to life. He always leads you in the way of truth. He always has your good in mind (meaning anything that makes you more like Christ, even if it's painful or not what you expected). He always has God's glory in mind, shaping your life into something that brings God honor and builds His kingdom.

Sweet friend, if you walk away from this chapter knowing anything, I hope it's this: the Holy Spirit is invaluable, indispensable, and fundamental. Yes, He automatically becomes a part of each of our lives when we accept Christ, but He's not one to be taken for granted or thought of as an add-on to life.

You may have questions at this point. Perhaps you're thinking, *This all sounds nice—the fact that the Holy Spirit is a person given to help, encourage, and sustain us. I get that He's absolutely vital to living a life of surrender. But how?*

Here are some of the incredible ways that the Holy Spirit has empowered me and helped me to navigate the surrendered life—and some ways He can help you too.

- **Understanding.** The Holy Spirit has helped me understand God's Word more fully and clearly. Jesus said in John 14:26 that the Holy Spirit will "teach you all things and bring to your remembrance all that I have said to you." He is our translator, to put it one way. He is our teacher and our reminder with the ability to help us discern what God's Word means. Psalm 119:105 tells us that God's Word is a lamp to our feet and a light to our path. If we are not rooted in the truths of God's Word, then how are we to walk without stumbling? How are we to navigate through the darkness of the world? How are we to live the Luke 9:23 life? The answer is to stay in step with the Spirit, to rely on His help and His ability to reveal the Scripture, our trusted guidebook, to us.

- **Conviction.** The Holy Spirit has convicted me, whether I like to admit it or not, when I have tried to regain control over my life and failed to trust God's plan. In John 16:7–8 Jesus told His disciples about "the Helper," that is, the Holy Spirit. Not only was He purposed to be the believer's helper and guide, but He was also purposed to "convict the world concerning sin and righteousness and judgment." It's hard to admit that we're in the wrong. It's even harder to forsake our false beliefs, sins, and rebellious attitudes toward God. But the fact that the Holy Spirit is also our conviction is good news. It is completely loving, gracious, and merciful of God to give us a chance to turn back to Him. It is completely overwhelming in the best ways, that He would give us the Holy Spirit to nudge us and say, *Hey, you're not living the life I called you into when you were saved, so repent. Return to Me.* When it comes to living the surrendered life, you can bet the Holy Spirit will convict us if we are grasping too tightly to personal control instead of trusting our Father. No matter how much it may hurt, no matter how hard or how long it may take to accept this conviction, it is truly one of the most loving acts from God because He wants nothing but the best for us—and that means turning away from what we want and settling into His better plan.

Here are some practical disciplines to help you walk by the Spirit daily and surrender to His leading:

- **Read your Bible.** Daily spending time immersed in God's Word will help you learn the Holy Spirit's voice. John 16:13 tells us that the Spirit was sent to guide us into all truth. One of the Holy Spirit's main jobs is to give us discernment and understanding not only in our Bible reading but in our everyday lives. Whether we're confused or curious, the Spirit illuminates the truth of God's Word to our hearts. He's not out to confuse but to clarify, and because He does so, we are able to walk by the Spirit in truth.
- **Pray often, in faith.** Ask the Holy Spirit to reveal Himself powerfully to you. Ask the Holy Spirit to give you peace about decisions or circumstances that may arise in your life. Keep a line of open communication with Him throughout the day. The more time we spend with Him in prayer, with thanksgiving, requests, and supplication, the more we get to know Him.
- **Repent of your sins daily.** Do not neglect the conviction of the Spirit, but confess your sins daily, allowing the Lord to take control and replace the spirit of your old flesh with your new, Christ-centered one.
- **Practice the fruits of the Spirit** and let them be evidenced in your life. Walking by the Spirit means cultivating healthy fruit in our life. Proof of a surrendered life is walking at Jesus' pace and emulating the fruit He produced.

I'm also a big fan of finding key verses to encourage reliance on the Spirit. You can memorize them (a great way to make sure they're always on hand) or you can write them on cards to post around the house where you're likely to see them. Whatever your strategy, keeping biblical truths top of mind is a practical way to stay on the path of surrender. Here are a few of my favorites:

- "But the Helper, the Holy Spirit, whom the Father will send in my name, he will teach you all things and bring to your remembrance all that I have said to you." (John 14:26)
- "And I will put my Spirit within you, and cause you to walk in my statutes and be careful to obey my rules." (Ezekiel 36:27)
- "Teach me to do your will, for you are my God! Let your good Spirit lead me on level ground!" (Psalm 143:10)
- "Likewise the Spirit helps us in our weakness. For we do not know what to pray for as we ought, but the Spirit himself intercedes for us with groanings too deep for words." (Romans 8:26)
- "But the fruit of the Spirit is love, joy, peace, patience, kindness, goodness, faithfulness, gentleness, self-control; against such things there is no law." (Galatians 5:22–23)

There is only one who is qualified to teach us how to surrender our control and trust God and truly sustain that way of life. Not-so-spoiler alert: It's God. Your heavenly Father. His living and active presence is manifested in the Holy Spirit. He's not some cryptic, far-off ghost just floating around aimlessly. Rest, dear one, knowing that He is with you, even now.

Space to Surrender

> But the fruit of the Spirit is love, joy, peace,
> patience, kindness, goodness, faithfulness,
> gentleness, self-control; against such things
> there is no law.
>
> GALATIANS 5:22–23

1. Where are you in your relationship with the Holy Spirit?
2. Not everyone experiences the Holy Spirit in the same way, but it's important to know Him as your helper and power source. List some of the ways you've experienced the Holy Spirit's leading, presence, or help in your life.
3. Maybe you feel super familiar with the Holy Spirit, or maybe the idea of having a relationship with Him is completely new territory. Wherever you are in that journey, write a prayer to the Holy Spirit, asking for a closer relationship with Him.

Holy Spirit, I realize that I cannot do anything without Your help. I believe You're my power source. Sometimes it seems impossible to surrender my story to God, but I believe the next step is always possible when I'm walking in Your power.

CHAPTER 6

God's Will 101

God is God. If He is God, He is worthy of
my worship and my service. I will find rest
nowhere but in His holy will, and that will is
infinitely, immeasurably, unspeakably beyond
my largest notions of what He is up to.

ELISABETH ELLIOT

ONE OF THE MOST DIFFICULT and frustrating realities of living with fibromyalgia is that you never know when a flare-up will rear its ugly head. On Monday I might be feeling like a million bucks with minimal pain and lots of energy to complete my to-do list for the day. But by the time the sun rises on Tuesday, a switch could flip. Unlike the day before, I might find myself in bed, unable to move for hours or even days. And when a flare-up hits, sleep, movies, heat packs for pain, and food are suddenly the *only* things on my to-do list—throwing my week off and resulting in a bunch of canceled plans.

Over the last eight years, this unpredictable illness has forced me to miss out on quality time with friends, numerous church services and events, dates with my boyfriend/husband, flights, work-related trips, and more. And full disclosure: as this uncertainty became more of a frequent reality in my life, I started to have some serious questions about "God's will." These questions weren't exactly new, but my illness forced me to confront two things I believe everyone struggles with when it comes to God's will: suffering and uncertainty. Suffering tempts us to question the goodness of God's will. And uncertainty—whether about big life plans or the next step—forces us to choose between genuinely trusting God or continuing to pursue the myth of control.

Here's how that played out in my own life.

In Suffering

The idea of God's will was something "nice and churchy" that I heard about regularly when I was growing up. Those two words were casually mentioned in the lyrics of my favorite worship songs or during conversations with loved ones.

"Just follow God's will for your life."

"God's will over mine."

But at the peak of my illness, when it was the hardest and most painful, when all my body could do was lie at home and miss out on life, those kinds of phrases tormented me.

Why would God allow me to suffer? Why would God's will include saddling me with a chronic illness? Why would God's plan involve me missing out on the life a typical teenage girl should be living? Beyond those specific questions, I was really wrestling with a pretty fundamental question about God: If God loves His children, why doesn't He make life easy and light for us?

Chances are, you have your own set of "Why would God" questions.

Why would God not fulfill my desire to have a boyfriend or be married?

Why would God let mental illness plague my life, day in and day out?

Why would God allow my parents to finalize their divorce?

Why would God put me in such a hard job and work environment?

Why would God not grant my good desire to have children of my own?

Why would God let my loved one get sick or die?

Why would God allow a pandemic to shut down the world and affect millions?

Sweet friend, I wish I could spend this entire chapter answering every single one of your "Why would God" questions. But as much as I wish that for us, it's not possible. Nor would it be good for us! If our willingness to trust and follow God is based on demanding that He explain and justify all the parts of life that we don't like, that wouldn't be faith at all.

Before I was diagnosed with fibromyalgia, it seemed easy to say I was trusting God and surrendered to His will. Life had been smooth sailing for as long as I could remember. Academics, athletics, friendships, and day-to-day life just came so effortlessly to me. It sure seemed like God had lined up all the cards in my favor. But when life began to do what it does best—throw us for a loop—the idea of "God's will over my own will" suddenly wasn't so easy to embrace.

In Uncertainty

If you were to do a quick Google search for "Bible verses about God's will," you might be surprised at the results. As you first type those words into the search bar, you may be hopeful—*surely the Bible will have a lot of obvious things to say about God's will.* Well, after scanning through a few blog posts and articles, you may find yourself stumped, with a once-hopeful smile quickly turning into a furrowed brow and confused sigh.

That's how I felt a few years ago. When—thanks to my mentor confirming the Holy Spirit's rumblings in my heart to pursue ministry—I decided to enroll online at a Bible college, and I felt like I finally had some semblance of direction. Heading back to college made me feel like I was finally getting my life back on track. I was finally doing something "serious" with my life.

But even with this newfound sense of direction, there were plenty of question marks. For example, I chose biblical counseling as my major—but truthfully, I wasn't quite sure where a counseling degree would take me or even why I felt the tug to pursue counseling rather than one of the other options. In my younger years, there was this air of shame associated with counseling and therapy. It felt like a taboo topic because going to counseling made it seem like you were a messed-up person in need of help. And that was just not a good look to the world around you.

(News flash: We're all messed up people in need of help. We're all sinners in need of a Savior.)

But after I was diagnosed with fibromyalgia, my family and I couldn't help but notice that the traumatic effects extended to every aspect of my life. That was when my parents and pastor recommended I meet with a counselor. At first I shut the idea down, insisting that I had it figured out. That I just needed time. But it wasn't only my body that had been affected—I was feeling emotional, spiritual, and mental fatigue.

When I started my biblical counseling classes, I was reminded of all the beautiful fruit that God brought from my own personal time in biblical counseling, a type of counseling that emphasizes that genuine and lasting change, healing, and hope are found in God's sufficient Word. Biblical counseling also prioritizes discipleship as an integral part of the Christian life. Because of what God had done in my life through counseling, I was excited to study it in school.

It sounds like the story could pretty much write itself from there—all wrapped up in a nice bow. *And Tara went on to study biblical counseling without any further doubts or questions, and began a long, successful career in her new calling. The end.*

But that's not how it played out. It's true—I did feel as if God had opened the door to online Bible school with a bright neon sign that said YES! However, I would be lying if I said I never questioned God or His will along the way.

You see, it doesn't matter if life is going well or if life is going poorly. Every now and again, we all stop, pause, and wonder, "Am I really supposed to be here? Is this God's will for my life? Am I making decisions that God would approve of?" That's where that pesky Google search comes in. I can't tell you how many times I paused during those first few semesters of biblical counseling school, combing through the internet and the Bible for any hints about God's will.

Was I on the right track? Was I really doing what God wanted, or was I messing up my life by following my own will? The lines were beginning to blur. Uncertainty was everywhere. After each Google search and scavenger hunt through the Bible, hoping to discover specifics about God's will for my life, I felt more defeated. Why was God's will so ridiculously hard to figure out? If it's so important to our lives, then why didn't He make it more obvious?

Just in case no one has told you before—it's okay to admit that you've had those same thoughts. Whether suffering has made you question whether you really want to follow God's will or uncertainty has you feeling as if there's no hope of even knowing what God's will is, much less following His will, this chapter is for you. It's time to grab our shovels and dig deep into what the Bible says about God's will. It's time to get our hopes up when it comes to God's will. It's not the time to shrink back in fear.

God wants to be known. He wants His will for us to be known. He's given us His Word to give us insight into His will. And when we understand the beauty of God's will, we're able to take another step toward surrender—even in the face of suffering or uncertainty.

God Keeps Secrets

If I were to ask you what book of the Bible is the least interesting to you, what would your answer be? There are a few that come to my mind (just being honest here), but if I had to give you one answer it would have to be the book of Deuteronomy. Don't get me wrong: I absolutely adore reading the Old Testament. But there's something about the book of Deuteronomy that used to make me feel confused and intimidated.

But in my quest through the Bible to define God's will, I realized something. One of the most important verses that gives insight on God's will is found in the middle of Deuteronomy, my least-read book. God gently and powerfully reminded me that every single word in the Bible is valuable, useful, life-giving, and breathed out by Him (2 Timothy 3:16–17).

Read Deuteronomy 29:29 with me: "The secret things belong to the LORD our God, but the things that are revealed belong to us and to our children forever, that we may do all the words of this law."

Let's backtrack for a moment. To understand this verse, we need to look at the book of Deuteronomy as a whole. Deuteronomy is about the renewal of the covenant that God had made with Israel years and years earlier, and it was written to remind the Israelites of how important God's holy standards were.

To give you the short, summarized, CliffsNotes version of the original covenant, it was essentially an agreement God entered into with His people. Israel promised to obey all God's commands, and God promised to guide, protect, and bless the people of Israel. In typical Old Testament fashion, Moses took blood from an animal and sprinkled it on the people—not as an excuse to be morbid but as a symbol of cleansing and atoning. Think of the blood as a way of linking the altar and the Israelites, symbolizing the union of God and Israel through the covenant they had made.

Now, circle back with me to Deuteronomy 29. Forty years had passed since the original covenant, and God saw a need for His people to be reminded. The covenant needed to be renewed. Just as your driver's license needs to be renewed every so often, God saw fit to use His servant Moses to remind Israel of their former commitment to God. (Raise your hand if you need a daily reminder of God's Word too!) You see, most of the generation that was sprinkled with blood forty years before were dead, and there was a new generation on the scene. They'd only heard about the covenant secondhand, so it was time for a reminder and new commitment.

After Moses reiterated God's covenant with the newer generation, he paused in verse 29 to share a principle of how God speaks to His people and some basics about how to understand His will. This conversation continued far after chapter 29, but God purposefully put it on Moses's heart to stop in the middle of what he was saying and relay these six important truths about God's will in one verse.

1. **God doesn't declare everything to mankind.** There are some things He keeps close to His heart in secret. But this shouldn't tempt our hearts to distrust Him: He has the right to have secrets because, well, He is God.

2. **God does declare some things to mankind.** The fact that God loves His people, desires for them to obey His commandments, and is always present in their lives tells us He is not silent. He has a message to share, and He deeply desires His people to know it. Given that reality, God's people have the responsibility to pay close attention to what He has to say.

3. **God's revelation always intends to say something to us.** "God's revelation" is another way to say God's will. He wouldn't be a very loving God if He spoke only to tickle our ears. Instead, we can stake our lives on the fact that there is a message that *does* belong to us.

4. **God's will is generational.** God intended some messages in His Word for only certain people. Some of what God spoke

in the Bible was meant for the context and culture of a certain time. But there are some passages we can also apply to our lives! This message about God's will had implications and applications not only for the second-generation Israelites but also for you and me today. God's will and Word are eternal and timeless—giving insight, influence, and application to every generation past, present, and future.

5. **God's given will is eternal.** It doesn't just last for a few generations, but it lasts an eternity with everlasting significance. You can probably think of a few fads and trends that come and go in arenas like social media or fashion. But God's Word is not a sweeping and passing trend—it is timeless and true, regardless of the generation.

6. **God's will and Word always matter.** Again, He doesn't just speak to tickle our ears or satisfy our fleeting curiosity. He gives His will to affect the way we *live, speak,* and *act.* Just as James 1:22 says, we weren't created to be people who simply hear God but who *do* His will and *live* for Him.

If you were paying close attention to Deuteronomy 29:29, you may have noticed something: there are two different aspects to God's will. One aspect is revealed to us, but the other isn't as clear and is only in view for God. From where we stand, some things are made plain, but other things are kept secret.

You may be thinking, *Hold up. God's will already seems complicated enough. And now there are two different aspects I must consider?*

Here's the thing. God does not have two competing wills that contradict each other, and He doesn't go back on His word. There's consistency between God's hidden and revealed will—we just don't have the full picture. But we do have a partial picture, and that is what we are seeking in this chapter. And may I be bold enough to say that knowing there are two different aspects to God's will actually answers all of our questions?

The first will of God is called His "secret will," which we learn about in the first part of Deuteronomy 29:29. This may be a hard pill to swallow, but we need to rip the Band-Aid off hard and fast. Bottom line, no matter how hard we pray and ask God to reveal everything to us, there are things He does not intend for us to know. As one of my good friends puts it: "I think our brains would literally explode if we knew the secret will of God."

Now, hear this clearly: God's secret will, the things that belong to God and God only, is not an invitation to go on an elaborate scavenger hunt. Unfortunately, being good enough, wise enough, or smart enough will not grant us an all-access pass to the vault of God's secret will. It's not a puzzle we're meant to solve. Nor is it the next rung on a ladder for us to try and climb to. God told Moses to tell the Israelites—and us today—some things have only His name on them.

After learning about God's secret will, I was all over the place emotionally. In one moment, gratefulness and relief would wash over me. It was freeing to realize I'm not expected to know or understand everything. But the next moment, frustration and confusion would overcome me. I have always been the type who hates surprises. My close friends and family know that I never—and I mean *never*—want a surprise birthday party.

Whether you hate surprises like me or you thrive on suspense and thrill, I would guess that God's secret will is one surprise that is hard for you to accept. Honestly, the thought that God has withheld things from me—especially things that pertain to my life—has never sat well with me. For a long time, especially in the height of some of the serious trials in my life, I didn't want to accept that there are parts of God's plan for my life I couldn't unlock or understand.

You may be reading this and thinking there's really no upside or positive spin when it comes to the secret will of God. After all, wouldn't a loving God be generous with His revelation and will? Isn't withholding generally looked upon as a bad thing? As if we're being given the short end of the stick?

May I propose a couple reasons as to why a loving God would keep secrets from His children?

1. If we knew everything about God's plan and will for us, there would be no need to walk by faith. Second Corinthians 5:7 says, "For we walk by faith, not by sight." One day, when we are reunited with Jesus in heaven, there will be no need to walk by faith because we will see the presence of God with our very eyes. But for now, walking by faith is the important, joyful, and secure path we're called to tread. If every plan was laid out for us, there would be no need to depend on God. When I live and feel as if I know it all, I act like I am the god of my story. It's far too easy for me to become puffed up, falsely believing I am enough. But there is much more freedom and joy in trusting God one step at a time. Why? Because with God, the possibilities are endless. The hope He promises each one of us, not just in heaven, but in our day-to-day lives, is immeasurably more than we could ever imagine. You can bet your entire life on the fact that when you walk by faith, the Lord will give you everything you need.

2. Sometimes too much knowledge can be a burden—not for God but for us. Has anyone ever asked you, "If it were

possible, would you want to see your future?" The idea is tempting, sure, but ultimately it would prove to be too heavy for us to bear. Each of our stories holds inevitable heartaches, losses, and trials. Each also holds incredible joys, celebrations, and victories. But too much information for even the highest of IQs could be overwhelming, burdensome, and paralyzing. All of this knowledge could very well make it difficult to make decisions, move forward in faith, and even trust God. Romans 11:33 says, "Oh, the depth of the riches and wisdom and knowledge of God! How unsearchable are his judgments and how inscrutable his ways!" Find comfort knowing that the One who is the wisest, most knowledgeable, most powerful, and most loving is best equipped to direct our lives. He takes the burden away from us and frees us up to simply walk by faith, being held in His hand all the while.

> OUR JOB IS TO FOCUS ON THE THINGS GOD HAS REVEALED AND LIVE RESPONSIBLY, JOYFULLY, AND EXCITEDLY IN THE LIGHT OF WHAT HE'S GIVEN US.

So where does this leave us?

Our job is to focus on the things God has revealed and live responsibly, joyfully, and excitedly in the light of what He's given us. When we are content with what God has given us and fully trusting in His good and wise heart, we do not have to press for answers that God keeps secret. And that leads us to the second aspect of God's will: the revealed will of God.

God Holds Nothing Back

God's revealed will is found in the second part of Deuteronomy 29:29: "the things that are revealed belong to us and to our children forever."

We can easily get fixated on what God *hasn't* shown us—His secret will. God knows everything—so why does He leave us struggling with the burden of uncertainty? But when we take that approach, we ultimately miss what God *has* given us to know. We ask God to reveal His will for our lives, but we're too obsessed with discovering secrets instead of focusing on what He's given us.

Go back a few pages and read the six characteristics of God's will. God's revealed will can be defined in points 3 through 6: God's revealed will has a message for us, God's will is generational and eternal, and it gives us everything we need to live.

What God has revealed so generously to us is what we should be focusing on, day in and day out. When we focus on what God has given us, it will enable us to put more trust in God's hidden will. Think about it: when we set our eyes on what God has revealed to us, we can stop worrying about what He hasn't. The more we focus on God's revealed will, the more we can trust Him to take care of what we will never know. As strange as it sounds, it becomes a comfort.

I pray that God's will is starting to make a bit more sense now. I pray that the fog is starting to clear. But there are still two big elephants in the room.

The first elephant: Where do I learn about God's revealed will?

The second elephant: What is God's revealed will for me specifically?

Fear not, friend. God's Word holds all the answers. Are you ready to dig in?

WHERE DO I LEARN ABOUT GOD'S REVEALED WILL FOR MY LIFE?

Over the last four years or so, I have had the honor of being a leader for my church's middle school youth group. It's been one of my favorite ways to serve because I remember what a pivotal time sixth, seventh, and eighth grade was for me and my relationship with God.

I once taught a lesson on the history and importance of the Bible and left the group of thirty-five middle schoolers with quite the hefty goal. I challenged them to read the entirety of Psalm 119. For those who may not know, Psalm 119 is the longest chapter in the entire Bible, with a whopping 176 verses. What I asked was not for the faint of heart.

But what was the point? I wanted them to read what God's Word tells us about itself. King David wrote Psalm 119 to celebrate God's Word as the perfect guide for life. I challenged the students to take notes on how David described the Bible. One of my favorite examples is when David describes God's Word as a "lamp to my feet and a light to my path" (119:105). My goal was to get the wheels in their brains turning and help them think about what God's Word was able to do in their lives.

Friend, let's not mince words. All too often we overcomplicate this matter of discovering God's will. But God hasn't hidden what we need to know. It's not a scavenger hunt. It's not a rung on the ladder that only the "more spiritual" people can reach. Put plainly and simply, God's revealed will is found in His Word, ready for us to read, understand, and follow.

We are all walking the road of life. It's very possible to go about our lives and walk the road of life without direction. It's very possible to go about our lives walking in the dark, with only our hands out in front of us, shuffling along to make sure we don't run into anything. Many people walk the path of life like that. But the good news for the Christian is that God's Word is a lamp to our feet and a light to our path—enabling us to walk with confidence, not timidity.

Oftentimes when we are searching for God's will for our lives, the answer is right in front of us—in trusting His heart and His Word.

Here's how it works: God's revealed will includes something called His preceptive will. A precept is a command or principle that shows us exactly what God wants us to do or how He wants us to live. And where do we find those precepts? You guessed it: within the pages of the Bible.

Now, sure, there are other ways that we learn God's revealed will. He is not limited in how He teaches or reveals things to us. Many times He uses avenues like prayer and the counsel and advice of other believers. But the important thing to remember is that God's Word is the final authority. If someone were to give you counsel or advice that contradicts Scripture, then it should not be regarded as God's will for your life. If your feelings do not line up or remain true to God's precepts, then it's simply not God's will for your life. As you commit to making the precepts found in the Bible your guide for daily decisions, you will find yourself living right at the center of God's will for your life.

WHAT IS GOD'S REVEALED WILL FOR MY LIFE SPECIFICALLY?

Where I believe many of us get tripped up is when we think that God's revealed will is like a neon "this way" sign. When I encounter a tough decision or when I question the trajectory of my life, I naively think God will direct me to a passage in the Bible that will have my exact answer in big, flashing letters.

"Keep going to school."

"Marry him on this date, at this time."

"Go to the grocery store at 10:00 A.M. instead of 2:00 P.M."

We're very specific people. Most of us want to know the who, what, when, where, why, and how. Down to the exact letter, down to the exact second. But the hard truth we must embrace is that God's Word does not tell us whether we should be a doctor or a lawyer. His Word doesn't tell us if we should go to private school or public school. His Word doesn't tell us which grocery store to shop at. His Word doesn't tell us if we should go to Chick-fil-A or In-N-Out Burger for lunch.

That may be frustrating and disappointing. Isn't God a God of the details? Yes, yes He is. But we're focusing on the wrong details. In God's revealed will, He has given us principles to follow.

When it comes to our jobs, He's given us principles in His Word to follow that will lead us in making the right career decisions.

When it comes to who we should marry, He's given us characteristics to look for in a future spouse—one who is a fellow believer (2 Corinthians 6:14), whose life exhibits the fruits of the Spirit (Galatians 5:22–23), and so on.

Whatever situation you're in right now, know that God's Word has something to say about it. Do you remember truths 5 and 6 about God's will? It is *eternally timeless* and *meaningful*, impacting not only the original audience but also you and me today. It doesn't matter what century we're living in—God's Word is timeless and true. This should bring us so much comfort, knowing that although it may not tell us everything about specific situations, it does give us principles for how to live in those circumstances and honor God with everything we are and everything we do.

Godly Decision-Making 101

As we close out this chapter, I want to leave you with a practical, biblical guide for how to make God-honoring decisions in your life. No one is exempt from making choices and decisions. I bet you can think of a decision—whether about a relationship, a career, or something else—that you're faced with this very second.

If you're paralyzed by making a decision or fearful to commit to one path or another because it may not line up with God's will, consider these points.

- **Ask yourself if this decision will glorify God.** Meaning, will this choice bring honor to Him? Does this decision align with His Word? Does this option affirm Scripture or go against Scripture? Is it a sin?
- **Pray and never give up.** Speaking from personal experience, I can tell you that prayer is often underestimated. And yet it's one of the most emphasized themes in Scripture. Prayer is our connection to the heart of the Father and our way of communicating. It's not just a time for us to ask things of God but to listen. Through humble prayer, God speaks to us if we're listening and reveals truths in Scripture that guide us in making the right decision.
- **Seek guidance from wise counsel.** Whether that be a mentor, spouse, close friend, or pastor, never neglect advice from the body of Christ. The Bible stresses, over and over, the importance of godly community and the unity of the body of Christ. Think of someone in your life who is spiritually mature and theologically sound. Inviting them into your life and sharing your struggles not only builds intimacy and

trust, but it also provides an opportunity for God to use them to speak to you.

- **Consider your spiritual gifts.** The Father has gifted us all in unique ways, for His glory and for specific purposes. How He has gifted us is a significant part of our purpose and the way He's intended us to serve, work, and relate. Remember, everything has potential to glorify the Lord (1 Corinthians 10:31). God wants you to use your giftings, and He often lines those up with your vocation, relationships, and so on.

- **Step out in faith.** Don't be afraid if you're at a crossroads between multiple good decisions—a variety of options that all honor the Lord and do not contradict His Word. Let's not forget that God has given us free will and free choice. He didn't come to save and have a relationship with mindless robots. He wants disciples who genuinely desire to follow Him and obey Him. The fact that God gives us real choices is a great opportunity to rely on Him more to make our decisions in life. Don't be afraid to take a step in faith if God has presented you with multiple options. We are not powerful enough to mess up what God has for us. Rest assured that if we make a wrong decision, He will surely redirect us if we're obedient and in tune with Him. He wastes nothing, friend, and when your mind and heart are aligned with what He's revealed, you have freedom to move forward in faith and confidence.

> WE ARE NOT POWERFUL ENOUGH TO MESS UP WHAT GOD HAS FOR US.

Abide in the True Vine

You're probably wondering if I ever figured out whether I should continue studying biblical counseling at college. To answer your question, I still have not figured out if that's something God wants me to continue, pause, or stop entirely. While I am writing this, I have completed half of the degree program and am taking a break due to God opening the door to writing books and focusing on being a new mama.

Honestly, I don't know what God's will is for me in this particular area. But may I tell you one thing I know for certain?

God hasn't hidden what I need to know. God hasn't hidden what He wants us, His beloved children, to know. And if we remain connected to the True Vine (John 15), we will find ourselves abiding, thriving, and being continually sanctified.

There's no surer place to live each day and face the decisions as they come. There's no greater sense of confidence. Knowing all of this helps you and me release our control. The fact that we're equipped with God's precepts but not provided with every specific detail of His plans and purposes is an invitation to surrender our steps to the One who knows it all and has given us all we need.

Space to Surrender

Your word is a lamp to my feet
and a light to my path.

PSALM 119:105

1. Write down one or two decisions that you are currently faced with in your life. Oftentimes, acknowledging them in this way helps us surrender them to God.
2. Do you find waiting for answers easy or hard? Why?
3. Spend some time brainstorming how you can support other members of the body of Christ when they are having a hard time discerning God's revealed will.

Heavenly Father, help me have the patience and trust to rest in Your plan for me, even if I don't know the full extent of it yet. Help me to walk in faith without worry.

CHAPTER 7

Walking at God's Pace

Jesus knows turns you never heard of, makes roads
you wouldn't have dreamed of, makes miracles
happen exactly where you never would have
imagined. There is a reason He is called the Way.

ANN VOSKAMP

THIS IDEA OF SURRENDERING OUR stories to God is vast, isn't it? Think of it like your favorite hiking trail. One of my favorite hiking spots is just minutes away from my childhood home. The beauty of this hike is not just its stellar views and waterfalls, but the fact that it has multiple diverging paths to explore, with each path leading to one grand destination: a beautiful cascading waterfall. The same goes for a life of surrender. There are many beautiful paths to explore that all lead to one destination: a place where we've learned how to release our death grip on control, and to surrender and trust God instead. We've explored the path of learning to trust God. We've walked along the trail of abandoning the idol of self-sufficiency. We've taken steps toward getting to know the Holy Spirit as our ever-present guide. We've discovered the freedom that comes when we stop overcomplicating the idea of God's will and embracing instead the simplicity of following His revealed precepts—knowing that if we live according to what He's revealed, we can step out with faith and confidence.

As we've journeyed through this book together, my hope is that these paths have not overwhelmed you with an endless to-do list or made you feel frantic about the surrendered life. Quite the opposite. My prayer is that as you've explored these paths, you've begun to gain a sense of peace, quieting the anxiety that always accompanies our efforts to control our destinies.

It's time for the next path along the way to surrendering our stories. And I must be honest: long before I even typed my first words of this book, I was looking forward to writing this chapter the most.

I have been the most challenged (and honestly, annoyed) by this path. This has been an especially hard gospel truth for me to embrace, and I suspect I'm not alone in this. And the fact that it's so difficult reveals just how important it is. We haven't shied away from the hard things so far, and we aren't going to start now.

Faster Isn't Always Better

I can't tell you how many times I've asked God this very question (sometimes in the most disrespectful tone): "Now what?"

I've sighed, shaken my head, and thrown my hands up in frustration more than I'd like to admit. I know at my very core that the life abundant Jesus promised in John 10:10 is not control but surrender. I know, deep in my gut, that Jesus doesn't give oppressive restrictions but life-giving commands.

Although my head and gut know all of this to be true, my heart doesn't always seem to agree. I've been tempted on more than one occasion to believe the lie that God is too slow. I've thought to myself, *If only God would let* me *have the steering wheel, things would go a lot faster.* Anyone else with me?

But faster doesn't always mean better. Another upside-down kingdom truth is that God doesn't operate on our schedules or timelines but on His. The kingdom of God runs on a different timeline—a heavenly timeline—that oftentimes seems (to us) to move at a snail's pace. Whether we realize it or not, we've been brainwashed to believe that faster *is* always better.

"Slowing down will kill you."

"Why wait when you can have it now?"

When we start to believe the lie that we would be better off—and further along—without God running the show, we miss the point of living the surrendered life. The cross-bearing, Jesus-following life (Luke 9:23). When we say yes to the beauty that is surrender, we also need to be prepared to wait. To be patient. To defer to another's timeline. To be content and trusting in the pace of God, rather than ours.

If you're like me and you've ever wondered why God was

taking so long with his plan for your life . . . if you've ever thought that life may be better or faster if you were in control . . . if you've ever wondered why patience takes up a lot of space in the Bible . . . lean in with me, friend.

It's time to walk at God's pace. It's time to learn His beautiful rhythm of patience.

The Three *P*'s: Pit, Prison, and Palace

Do you remember the adorable flannel boards your Sunday school teachers used to tell Bible stories when you were a kid? I totally feel nostalgic about flannel board story time. It was one of my favorite parts about each Sunday, sitting crisscross applesauce while the teacher told us a Bible story and stuck each character on the board. I was the kid who was absolutely mesmerized by how the story was illustrated and was always the first to volunteer to pin the felt characters and animals on the board for the entire class to see.

One of the most vivid memories I have of the flannel board includes an Old Testament Bible character. He is known for his coat of many colors and his ridiculous number of siblings—Joseph.

I began to realize, the more I studied his life, that Joseph's colorful coat was only a tiny fraction of his story. Sure, I get why Sunday school teachers primarily focused on that part of his life via the flannel board. It was pretty and fun. But if we look closer at Joseph's life, we can sum it up in three words—and the first two words aren't the most glamorous.

Pit.
Prison.
Palace.[6]

There's one common thread that connects each one of those words. Let's explore it and see what Joseph's unexpected path reveals.

#1: PIT

It all started with that darn coat and a father who played favorites among his children. Jacob loved Joseph, one of his twelve sons, the most, and he wasn't afraid to show it. Genesis 37:3 says, "Now Israel loved Joseph more than any other of his sons, because he was the son of his old age."

I'm sure we all know where this story is going. Inevitably, jealousy came knocking. Maybe you can relate to a little sibling rivalry. I know that my brother and I had our moments of competition and jealousy. Ninety-nine percent of the time it's harmless, right? Well, in this case, not so much. Jealousy led this band of brothers to come up with a downright devious plan: kill Joseph, lie to their dad, and go on living without their pesky, overachieving brother.

Talk about twisted, right? But thankfully, after some convincing from the oldest brother, Reuben, they decided to chill out a bit, lower the intensity level, and not kill him. Instead, they would just ambush him and throw him in a pit. I wish I could say this was just some ancient fraternity hazing that got a little out of hand, but the fact is, Joseph's brothers had become truly bitter. What happened next proves how much they hated Joseph.

#2: PRISON

After throwing Joseph in that dark pit, Joseph's brothers saw a caravan of not-so-friendly Ishmaelites in the distance, traveling toward Egypt. Looking to kill two birds with one stone—get rid of Joseph for good *and* make a little extra cash, Joseph's brothers gave him to these traders for a few pieces of silver. In a matter of hours, Joseph had gone from being the golden boy to a victim of human trafficking. This wasn't exactly what Joseph was expecting out of his life. Just a chapter before his brotherly betrayal, Joseph was given a dream from God Himself that He would raise Joseph up as a ruler over the nations. And now Joseph was being dragged to Egypt to face who knows what kind of cruel slavery? None of this made sense.

In Egypt Joseph found himself a victim of more injustice. Joseph was sold to Potiphar, a military leader who served as Pharaoh's captain of the guard. Things could have been worse. Joseph's master noticed that he was a hard worker and that everything he worked on became successful. Eventually, Potiphar put Joseph in charge of his entire estate and made Joseph his personal attendant and adviser. Not bad for a kid from the desert! But Potiphar had a wife who had all the heart eyes for Joseph. She tried her hardest to entice him, yet Joseph proved again to be an upright man of God. When attempts at seduction didn't work, vengeance seemed to be the next best plan. Poor Joseph wound up being accused of attacking Potiphar's wife and found himself in prison. Talk about a bad rap.

However, time and time again, we're told the Lord was with him, and Joseph became a successful man. Even though he was betrayed by his brothers, literally sold for money, and unjustly accused of rape, Joseph found favor with God and was blessed in this new life that he didn't choose or want. Although he was repeatedly derailed from the life God promised him, he waited. Incredible, supernatural patience was required of Joseph as decades of his life played out—all according to God's pace, not his own.

#3: PALACE

Time passed and Joseph was still in prison. Here was a young man who probably couldn't fathom where God was taking him. He had been betrayed. He had become a victim. He felt the weight of broken promises. No one would have blamed Joseph if he let depression and hopelessness overcome him. You and I may not have life stories like Joseph's (Who does? The guy has one of the craziest life stories I've ever read!), but we can all identify with those feelings of being filled with expectation about God's good plans for our lives, only to see things take an unexpected turn. Feeling disappointed, betrayed, and even angry is a common response when we've tried so hard to wait for God to come through, but it seems as if He is nowhere to be found.

We read in Genesis 41 that Joseph was given a second chance. Two of Pharaoh's servants, the chief baker and the cupbearer, were imprisoned for offenses they committed. One night as they awaited their fates, they both had dreams with two very different interpretations. Enter Joseph.

Because of the Lord's favor on Joseph, he was able to interpret the dreams. The dreams revealed the outcome of the two men's imprisonments: within a matter of days, the baker would be executed, but the cupbearer would be set free and welcomed back to the palace. The cupbearer was amazed and super grateful, so he promised Joseph to put in a good word with Pharaoh. But the cupbearer forgot all about Joseph, and Joseph remained in prison.

After *more* time passed with Joseph still in prison, God gave him another opportunity for freedom. This time his task was to interpret Pharaoh's troubling dreams. Hearing that Pharaoh was suffering from a recurring nightmare that none of his advisers could interpret, the cupbearer finally remembered Joseph

SURRENDER YOUR STORY

and what he'd promised. After years of suffering unjustly in total obscurity, Joseph found himself in the presence of the most powerful person in the world—and he was ready to step up. God blessed him with not only the interpretation of the dream (it turned out to be a warning about a terrible famine in the future) but also the wisdom to recommend a solution. Pharaoh respected Joseph so much that he gave him a permanent staff position—sort of like his role at Potiphar's estate but now on a *much* larger scale. The Pharaoh of Egypt could tell there was something different about Joseph. The "Spirit of God" was with him (v. 38).

And wouldn't you know it! After decades of injustice, betrayal, and things not going according to Joseph's plan, God fulfilled His promises. Joseph rose to become everything God had prophesied in his dream. God purposefully used patience to further Joseph's story, grow his trust in Him, and help him live surrendered to God's sovereign will, even if the timing and events didn't make sense.

Patience Is the Missing Puzzle Piece

How did you do? Were you keeping your eyes peeled for that common thread? You may be thinking that thread is the fact that each setting starts with the letter *P* (I love a good use of alliteration), but that's not quite it.

It may not come as a surprise to you, but Joseph is known as one of the most patient men in the Bible. Do a quick Google search or ask one of your favorite scholars to point out one of

Joseph's most prominent qualities, and they would likely tell you patience.

Think about each of the places where Joseph found himself: a pit, a prison, and eventually, a palace. What they all share isn't their accommodations, but the character of Joseph during his time in each place.

Patient. Enduring. Long-suffering.

In the pit, facing the betrayal of his brothers, physical pain, and the fear of a suddenly uncertain future—Joseph was patient.

In prison, wrongfully accused and most likely discouraged that God had not fulfilled His promises yet—Joseph was patient. He persevered.

In the palace he faithfully trusted the Lord and worked heartily, even though this wasn't the role he thought he was supposed to play.

Reading about Joseph's life often makes me feel guilty for complaining about anything in my life. But that's not the main message we should walk away with after reading Joseph's remarkable story. Nor should we just sit back and look with amazement at the fact that he survived the pit and accomplished so many great things, first at Potiphar's estate and then at Pharaoh's court, despite being sold into slavery when he was a seventeen-year-old barely out of puberty.

The heart of Joseph's story is patience. He waited for God to fulfill His promise that Joseph would be a leader of his people (Genesis 37:5–11). As he sat in the pit, as he waited in a prison cell, as he found himself so far removed from his family and betrayed by his own brothers, he held on to hope. He didn't try to manipulate his way out of his situation but instead patiently waited on God's perfect timing.

That's surrender. And Joseph's life shows us how patience is a vital piece to living the surrendered life.

If Joseph hadn't had patience, he could have very well interpreted the setbacks of his life as broken dreams and broken promises. But by faithfully exercising a habit of patient endurance—far beyond what most of us will ever have to endure on our journeys—he saw every setback as a stepping stone from his heavenly Father.

Things could have gone very differently for Joseph if he'd looked at God's seemingly crazy path and timeline and decided to distrust Him. Heck, I don't think anyone would blame him if he'd succumbed to hopelessness at *multiple* points in his life, from the first couple of hours in that pit to the years he languished in the Egyptian dungeon for a crime he didn't commit. He might well have had moments, hours, or days of struggling with despair. But ultimately, despair over his circumstances or disappointment in God didn't define his story or his destiny. With remarkable, supernatural patience, Joseph kept walking with God in faith, all the while trusting His power and plan.

So as we see illustrated so beautifully in Joseph's life, patience was the puzzle piece that God sovereignly placed in the picture to accomplish His purposes. Even if that meant Joseph had to go through hell and back. Even if it didn't make sense. Even if it took years and years and years.

And just as it was for God's servant Joseph, patience is still one of the main ingredients for walking faithfully *with God*. Without it, we simply cannot walk at God's pace. Without it, we will continue taking control and moving at a pace that leaves God and His good plans for us in the rearview. The momentary satisfaction of feeling like *now we're finally getting somewhere* when we're in control won't last.

Patience is God's way of enabling us to see the setbacks, disappointments, and delayed timing of our lives in a new light. In Him, through patience, we are freed up to live on heaven's timeline, one

> IN HIM, THROUGH PATIENCE, WE ARE FREED UP TO LIVE ON HEAVEN'S TIMELINE.

where there is no such thing as us getting the short end of the stick, because God is always on time, weaving our story into His glorious work.

Why Is It So Hard to Be Patient?

I have observed something about patience's evil twin, impatience. Maybe you can relate to what I've found. In our modern-day culture, impatience has started to disguise itself as something it isn't. I have seen it in my own life and the world around me, running around in a mask that hides its true self from view. Have you noticed that it's become easier and easier for us to camouflage our impatient hearts as "highly motivated" instead? Humanity has conjured up an excuse. Instead of calling impatience what it is, we say, "We're not impatient; we just know what we want."

In fact, impatience has been dressed up as a virtue, going by all kinds of names and phrases:

She's highly motivated.
So-and-so's such a go-getter.
"The hustle."

I'm sure you've heard this joked about: the younger generations (it started with millennials and continues with Gen Z) seeming to have a sense of entitlement that the older generations never had. That you can have anything you want, at any time, without working or waiting very long for it. That no one's a loser, everyone gets a first-place trophy. If you fall in one of those generational categories (hey, I'm a Gen Z-er over here!), I'm sorry. It's never fun being laughed at. (This is coming from one who occasionally has a hard time taking a joke.)

But may I make a bold declaration?

This is not just a millennial or Gen Z problem. It's a human problem.

It's a problem that's been around since sin entered the world. Do you remember why the world's first couple ate from the Tree of Knowledge of Good and Evil? They wanted to be like God. They wanted to take control. They wanted to get *what* they wanted *when* they wanted it. The fruit was there, and it was too shiny and delicious to wait. The potential of being like God and having their eyes enlightened was too alluring. In what I imagine to be a split second, a moment here then gone, Adam and Eve made their choice.

It seems fair to say that impatience played a role in Adam and Eve's decision to eat the fruit. They didn't want to wait and question if the snake was really telling the truth. And he played on their desires. Instead of resting in God's timing and provision, they took the shortcut Satan offered. They acted rashly based on what they felt in the moment instead of trusting what God had said.

I think we can relate to the world's first couple more than we'd like to admit. Patience is not natural. In fact, patience is supernatural. It's foreign to every single cell and muscle in our body. The idea of being patient will always evoke a response, whether an eye roll, a grimace, or a churning feeling in the pit of your stomach, because it's foreign to us.

But do you remember God's plan for sanctification? For His children to be made holy, to become more like Him through the Spirit's work in our lives? Sanctification is required because, as we all know, patience, among many other things in our lives, is uncomfortable and challenging. It's a constant struggle. It seems nearly impossible. But shall I share some more good news?

It's actually not impossible, despite what our flesh screams at us each day. I'm not saying it's the easiest thing in the world and we should just suck it up because it's a command from God. Yes, it *is* a command from God, and we should take that to heart and react in obedience. But there are two additional realities here, benefits and glimmers of hope when it comes to patience.

We don't have to produce patience on our own. The reason patience seems so hard is because we often try to accomplish it in our own strength. We try and inevitably fail because, as I said earlier, it goes against our natural wiring to wait for good things. Becoming truly patient takes supernatural help. I'm not just talking about the kind of patience that calculates that "things will work out better for me tomorrow if I wait today." I'm talking about the kind of patience that's willing to surrender to God's timing and direction even when you're in a Joseph-level crisis, when you weigh the costs and think, *Nope, there's no way this fits into my journey.* We become impatient. We start distrusting God when His timing seems slow or when we're forced to wait. But patience was never meant to be just a "me" thing or a "you" thing. Patience is part of the sanctifying work that God does in each one of His children. And whenever we talk about sanctification, we're talking about the involvement of the Holy Spirit, making us more like Jesus, who was the greatest example of the One who is patient. Sanctification is hard, but we don't have to do it on our own. God is waiting to teach us His pace, His way of life.

Additionally, patience is a virtue that will make us happier, more joyful, and more content here and now. Yes, there's an element of "already but not yet" that we need to keep in mind. Some of the blessings we receive through patience might be a long way off—and I'm talking about on-the-other-side-of-the-resurrection-in-heaven long way off. Patience isn't just some life hack for making all your dreams come true. Let me tell you, patience does have beauty and benefit for our lives right here and right now. We don't have to wait to experience it until we reach the gates of heaven.

Here's what I mean. Patience brings a radical perspective shift. Instead of basing our happiness, peace, joy, or contentment on our current circumstances (which are incredibly fleeting and fragile), you and I can look forward with hope. Think of hope and patience as supporting characters in a movie: they work hand in hand to create a beautiful screenplay.

In our walk with Christ, patience is the stunning supporting character that enables us to have peace and contentment today, right now, *even when life isn't what we thought.* Consider that if your criteria for being happy, peaceful, or joyful is your life being exactly what you wanted every moment of every day, you're ultimately setting yourself up for a disappointing experience. Life is imperfect and messy and incomplete. We're never "there" (whatever your "there" may be). We're *here*, constantly on a journey and in the middle of God's process. That's just the truth. Sometimes God's grace gives us what feels like a perfect moment—a beautiful sunrise, your baby's first smile, a dreamy proposal, an achievement you've been waiting your whole life for, or some other episode that feels like life couldn't be better.

But then we're back to the good but not-so-easy reality of our in-process lives.

Here's a little secret: those "perfect moments" are like glimpses of our heavenly home. Use them well—not to think, *Too bad my life isn't like this all the time*, but instead to thank God that this path of sanctification is leading us somewhere simply beautiful. Hope plus patience allows us to take joy in the journey, even those unexpected paths along the way. Patience is what lets you experience joy and peace not only in those glimpse-of-heaven moments but also in the normal times and, yes, even the difficult times. I guarantee you that patient people experience *way* more joy than those who are always living with impatient discontentment. Patience gives us the ability to trust the Lord, believing that God is in control and guiding us toward a wonderful destination, even when we're facing those pit or prison moments.

If you're anything like me, you think that sometimes those realities sound a bit too good to be true. If you're nodding your head in agreement, I have something wonderful to tell you. That's one of the marvelous things about our God. He isn't too good to be true—He's everything He says He is and more. And everything He calls us to do, including living a life of patience, is possible for us. But don't just take my word for it.

Following God's Timetable

"But the fruit of the Spirit is love, joy, peace, *patience*, kindness, goodness, faithfulness, gentleness, self-control; against such things there is no law" (Galatians 5:22–23, emphasis added).

Patience is one of the fruits of the Spirit, and yet we gloss over it. We read Galatians 5, rattle off the nine godly attributes, close our Bibles, go about our days, and completely miss the mark. God divinely inspired this list of the fruits of the Spirit through the pen of the apostle Paul, not just to take up extra space in the letter to the Galatians but to make a point. To encourage and enable life-change and transformation.

When I read that list, I think God is trying to drive home a point: Christians shouldn't just play defense, avoiding the bad stuff. They should also play offense, going after a goal. The Holy Spirit is our helper who helps us defend against sin, but He also enables us to play offense, going after the goal of producing godly characteristics in our lives.

This is where the fruits of the Spirit come in! And they're all modeled after the life of—you guessed it—Jesus Christ, our ultimate example. It should come as no surprise that patience was one of the attributes God wanted us to practice and produce, because Jesus' own life and example is completely characterized by patience.

I just love to nerd out on Scripture because it adds so much more depth to our lives, so let's look at the Greek word for *patience* used in Galatians 5.

Hupomone means

- patient enduring,
- waiting for, and
- properly remaining under.

I'll never forget one of my most played songs on my iPod Shuffle back in the day. It was a 1960s hymn covered and redone by Jars of Clay. The chorus went a little something like this: "And they'll know we are Christians by our love, by our love. Yeah, they'll know we are Christians by our love."[7] Is that jogging anyone else's memory?

That song is based on Jesus' own words to His disciples at the Last Supper: "By this everyone will know that you are my disciples, if you love one another" (John 13:35 CSB). But we could also sing, "And they'll know we are Christians by our *patience*."

Whether you're talking about love, patience, or any of the other fruits of the Spirit, these qualities are meant to set us apart from the world—to demonstrate that we belong to God. To display His character. And patience is one of those especially noticeable defining characteristics in this age of hustle culture. Patience is not just something we do when we're waiting for our order to be ready at Starbucks and running late for work. It's not just something we do when we're waiting to hear back about a new job or hoping for that engagement ring or waiting to hear if we got accepted into college.

The fruit of patience shows we are following God's plan and timetable rather than our own. In other words, when we endure (*hupomone*) and wait rather than rush ahead of God, we demonstrate that we have abandoned our own ideas of how the world should work and instead have surrendered to our sovereign Father who holds the whole world in His hands. Patience is ultimately expressed through our surrendered heart, acknowledging that God alone holds and controls not only the universe but also our lives—and that even includes the timing of how things will play out.

When I was growing up, my parents would often sing the church nursery rhyme "Be Patient" to my brother and me. Most of the time, they didn't sing it just to be funny. They sang it because they noticed something stirring inside their children. They noticed that we were relying too much on the world and our external circumstances and not the Lord and the internal work He desired to do in us.

As time went on, instead of being patient, my impatient heart demonstrated that I was putting my hope in something else other than my Savior.

My hope was in *my* schedule and *my* plans for the future. My hope was in *my* circumstances turning out the way *I* wanted.

But, as you can most likely relate to, when my hope is placed anywhere but in Christ, everything else crumbles. When I am impatient, it demonstrates a lack of contentment, faith, and trust in God and His promises. It becomes all too easy for me to dwell on what I consider disappointments and setbacks in my story, instead of believing that God has a beautiful purpose in the waiting.

Let's be honest. We all know, deep down in our guts, that patience is a virtue. We know to some extent that it's better to be patient than impatient. But *how*?

It's time to get practical, my friend. And not the kind of practical that you'll get from a generic self-help book, but from the source of all truth and life transformation.

Remember Your Power Source

Where does your power come from? Who is the One who empowers you to do the things you do? Who is the One who enables you to even get up every morning, breathe in, breathe out, and live? If your answer is yourself or a spouse or someone else, then maybe go back and read about the Holy Spirit again.

Somewhere along the way, we have started to call the fruits of the Spirit "fruits of Tara" or "fruits of Josh" or "fruits of (insert your name here)." Yes, you and I are supposed to produce and display these fruits in our own lives, but as we've learned, we cannot even begin to do that on our own. Patience is a fruit and result of the *Holy Spirit*, our power source, our helper, our teacher, our guide. Let's not miss the Spirit part.

Every once in a while, I share a Q&A box on my Instagram stories, opening up the floor to any and every question. Each time, without fail, someone asks a question about patience. Someone is struggling with being patient—knowing that we're supposed to in Christ—but they can't seem to hack it. Friend, you're not alone. Patience is hard. It's grueling. It's difficult. But may I offer some hope?

Patience is possible when we rely on the Holy Spirit. When we remember who our power comes from. Patience cannot be our natural instinct without Christ, but it can be our supernatural instinct when we remain connected to the True Vine. The great news is that we live in the power of another.

Right after Paul listed the fruits of the Spirit, he said to "keep in step with the Spirit" (Galatians 5:25). Simply put, this means to walk in a line behind a leader. When you are struggling to be patient, when you are tempted to rush ahead of God's timing and take the steering wheel, remember where you belong: behind the Spirit, walking in His steps. In the safety of God's will.

When you follow the Spirit, you don't have to worry for a second where He's taking you. You don't have to question His pace and His timing. You don't need to rush to the head of the line and tell God, "Step back. Follow me. I know better than You." Why? Because He is sovereign above all. He's in control. He's trustworthy. He has had everything figured out before time even began. And most of all, He loves you.

So here are three simple things you can do today to remain connected to the Spirit:

1. Every morning, wake up first thing and confess out loud, "Holy Spirit, lead me today." Admitting in prayer that we

need help is the first step, and let me tell you—God will not hesitate to come and answer that request.

2. Take time to read your Bible each day because, spoiler alert, that is the greatest way God speaks to us. If we're not hearing from the Lord and saturating ourselves in truth, we won't know how to walk. We'll be tempted to walk at our own pace instead of following God's. Not only is devoting time in your busy day to hearing from God an important way of expressing patience (building your time around a spiritual discipline) but it actually helps you become patient (and all the other fruits of the Spirit) when you're filling your mind with God's truths rather than your own thoughts and the voices of the world.

3. Examine your life and cut back on anything that is distracting you from the Lord. Maybe it's something like Instagram, Netflix, or food. When our lives are cluttered and we're consumed by the things of this world more than our Creator, we put up barriers to communicating clearly with the Spirit. He's too good and too wise to compete for our affections. Begin decluttering your life so that the Holy Spirit does not get shouted over.

Keep Your Eyes on the Prize

One of my favorite passages in the Bible is found in Hebrews, tucked away in chapter 12.

Therefore, since we are surrounded by so great a cloud of witnesses, let us also lay aside every weight, and sin which clings so closely, and let us run with endurance the race that is set before us, *looking to Jesus, the founder and perfector of our faith, who for the joy that was set before him endured the cross, despising the shame, and is seated at the right hand of the throne of God.* (vv. 1–2, emphasis added)

Ah, how we've overcomplicated it. The use of the word *race* in this passage gives us an amazing mental picture. Comparing our lives in Christ to an endurance race tells us a few things:

1. Life is not a quick sprint but a marathon that lasts a lifetime.
2. Life requires endurance and patience.

To me, long-distance running sounds a lot like death, but others find so much joy in it. One time I asked my cousin what helped him push through the fatigue and pain after his first triathlon. His response struck a chord with me: "What gets me through is knowing what I'm running toward. What gets me through is knowing my end goal."

We've all heard the saying, "Keep your eyes on the prize." Whoever came up with that was onto something. Hebrews 12 tells us that there will be weights and sin that drag us down in life. But to run the life Christ has given us with excellence and endurance, we have to keep our eyes on the prize. We must *look to Jesus and His example.* This is the key to having patience.

Our Savior is the ultimate example of one who endured the cross. But not just for any old thing: for the cross. For us. In his book *The Ruthless Elimination of Hurry*, John Mark Comer mentions that Christians are essentially apprentices of Christ. We're to emulate His lifestyle, His way of living. That's exactly what we need to be doing. We need to look to Jesus' actions.

What did He do? He kept His eyes on the prize. Jesus never did anything without looking heavenward—to His mission of saving us from sin. For us as finite, imperfect humans, keeping our eyes fixed on the future hope we have in Christ makes all the difference. Just like any good marathon runner, we need to keep the end goal in mind. If we focus on the temporary pain, setbacks, or timing of the race, we will falter. But looking to Christ, the author and perfector of our faith, changes everything.

If you want a perspective shift, not just in your pursuit of patience but in life, this is how.

ASK GOD FOR IT

I remember seeing a quote on Pinterest once that said something to this effect: "Prayer is our lifeline in times of trouble."

While that's a narrow way of understanding prayer—prayer isn't just for the hard times. Prayer is for *all* times (1 Thessalonians 5:16–18). So when we are struggling to be patient, when we are struggling to wait, one of the best things we can do is pray. We can ask God for His supernatural fruit of patience to bud, sprout, and thrive in our lives. It won't do us any good to sit around and wait for it to just magically appear. We must ask Him. In the middle of your day, when you're struggling to be patient—waiting for that test result, for a spouse, for a season of pain to end—ask God for patience. He wants to give His children good things. And patience is one of those good things, one of the best things, that He can't wait to give us.

GET HYPED. GET THANKFUL.

Lately my common response to something exciting is, "I'm hyped!" (Sorry to everyone who just cringed.) Today's culture has adopted this word too. Sure, it may sound cringey, but I think there's some wisdom to it when we think about how to practice patience.

The Christian should be the most excited, joyful, and hopeful person you meet. We have all the reason in the world to get our hopes up. And we have a responsibility to share that hope with others. So another practical way to produce patience is to anticipate (or get hyped about) what God has done and has promised to do for those who love Him. When we read God's Word and recall His promises to us, we can get excited. We can be hopeful. And that excitement and hope help us to be patient in our current seasons of waiting. We don't have to feel hopeless when things don't go our way or according to our timing, because we know that God keeps His good promises.

Along with anticipating all that God promises, practicing thankfulness also aids us in our pursuit of patience. First Thessalonians 5:18 tells us to "Give thanks in all circumstances; for this is the will of God in Christ Jesus for you." The apostle Paul could have let us all off easy and said, "Give thanks in *some* circumstances" or "Give thanks in *the easy* circumstances." Yet God was direct in His verbiage: "in *all* circumstances."

Impatience reveals that our heart is discontent and dissatisfied, whether about the timing of our lives or the results of our lives. So what's the antidote? Thankfulness. You may be saying, "Tara, there's nothing good in my life." I would beg to differ. The fact that you're alive and breathing is a reason to praise God. And our salvation in Christ is the best thing to be thankful for. If nothing else, start with thankfulness for your physical and spiritual life. And as you start thanking God for those fundamental blessings, I guarantee you will discover a few other things to be thankful for!

> THANKFULNESS IS THE KEY TO EASING ANY FEELINGS OF MISSING OUT— ANY FEELINGS OF IMPATIENCE AND DISSATISFACTION.

Thankfulness is the key to easing any feelings of missing out—any feelings of impatience and dissatisfaction. What practically helps me is writing down or speaking out loud a list of things I'm thankful for—big and small. Even when you don't *feel* particularly thankful, acknowledge what God has given you anyway. This trains our brains and hearts to give thanks in all circumstances. And when we do, we will start to find that God gives us contentment where we are now, with what we have now, instead of rushing ahead of His pace.

EMBRACE THE LESSONS ALONG THE WAY

There's always something to be learned, and this is no exception. Romans 5:3–4 tells us that the sufferings of life have a specific assignment and purpose from God—to produce endurance, character, and hope in us. How often do we skip over the seasons of waiting and rush past God because it's uncomfortable? Because it feels too slow?

But when we choose to be impatient instead of patient, we miss out on the refining work God has for us. We miss out on the opportunity to become more enduring people who are stronger in their character and hope. We miss out on the valuable soul work God intends to use to make us better—more holy, more sanctified.

So, friend, this is our challenge: to both embrace and celebrate the lessons along the way. To begin switching our mindset from *setback* to *lesson*. The world has started preaching there's no reason to wait, which couldn't be further from the truth. God has divine intention to turn everything we consider to be a slow setback into supreme sanctification.

Patience Is a Gift

Lest we ever forget: Patience is the secret to living with contentment here and now. Patience is the secret to having hope about the future, even if it doesn't look the way we thought, when we thought. Patience is the secret to being able to face the storms and struggles of life with grit and resilience and not succumb to discouragement.

A patient heart helps us step out of our demanding schedules and instead develop a God-centered schedule. A patient heart empowers us to release our death grip on control, knowing God's way is better than anything we could rush and manipulate on our own. Patience is choosing to love God enough to say, "Thank You" for the difficult things and "I trust You" even when He doesn't follow your timeline.

Space to Surrender

Not only that, but we rejoice in our sufferings, knowing that suffering produces endurance, and endurance produces character, and character produces hope, and hope does not put us to shame, because God's love has been poured into our hearts through the Holy Spirit who has been given to us.

ROMANS 5:3-5

1. Is there something in particular that you are having a hard time waiting for? How could you see God using this to sanctify you?
2. Our lives will inevitably have setbacks, but if we think of them as lessons, we are one step closer to growing in God's gift of patience. List some setbacks in your life that you were able to use as lessons and why.
3. What does it look like for you personally to walk at God's pace instead of your own?

Lord, You have so patiently walked beside me, even when I've tried to outpace You. I am grateful for Your presence through the Holy Spirit and ask that You grant me Your patient endurance.

CHAPTER 8

God's Résumé

Who can be compared with the Lord our God,
who is enthroned on high?

PSALM 113:5 NLT

ANYONE WHO KNOWS ME KNOWS that I'm quite the daddy's girl. Don't get me wrong, I love my mom. She is my person. But there's something to be said about the extra special connection a daughter has with her father.

When I was adopted at the wee little age of six months, my dad, Tom, was the one to pick me up from South Korea and bring me home. When the adoption agency gave my parents the green light to travel across the ocean to finalize my adoption, my mom and dad decided that one parent should stay home with Lee, my older brother, who had been adopted a year earlier. At that time he was almost two years old, and my parents wisely opted not to tote a toddler all the way to the other side of the globe.

And so my dad, my grandpa, and another local adoptive father packed their bags and flew across the ocean to bring home two Korean girls in need of homes. One being me and the other being my childhood best friend, who is like a sister to me.

From the moment my dad held me for the first time in Seoul, there was an instant connection. Even though we don't share the same DNA and even though we don't look alike at all, we are similar in so many ways. In fact, my husband, Michael, often jokes that I'm turning into a female version of my dad, and I can't help but laugh and agree.

My dad and I share the same love for corny jokes. We have the same sarcastic and goofy sense of humor. When it comes to cold, rainy days and the nostalgic joy of Christmas, we can't get enough. (Sorry. We are *those people* who listen to Christmas music and watch Christmas movies all year round.) If given the choice between a steak cooked medium well and a slice of birthday cake, we would both choose the steak without a second thought. And more times than not, my dad and I both tend to be constantly on the go—with the result that we struggle to rest, relax, and shut off our brains. Those are just a few of the uncanny similarities.

That being said, I've always known who my father is. I didn't just learn the small details about him like what he liked to order at our favorite Thai restaurant or his favorite color (beef and broccoli and blue, by the way). My knowledge of him goes way beyond his favorite ice cream flavor (vanilla, with my mom's homemade hot fudge) or what he likes to watch on television after a long day at work (likely a food or vacation home show). No, I have been blessed with a front-row seat to his life. I have been blessed to know the *real* Tom. His characteristics, qualities, beliefs, and values. Having him as my dad has given me the unique opportunity to witness the kind of person he is day in and day out. How he reacts in situations that are good and how he reacts in situations that are bad. How he treats others and what he truly values. How he loves God and how he strives to follow Him to the best of his ability.

A few moments especially stand out when I think about my dad. Ever since my mom was a young adult, she has struggled with some very intense, physical challenges and illnesses. I have lost track of how many surgeries she's had. But there's one incident that stuck with me because of what it showed me about my dad.

One afternoon when Lee and I were very little, my mom called us upstairs. There was a tone of urgency in her voice as we found her in the bathroom. She was cradling her elbow, explaining to us that a piece of bone had broken loose and locked up her joint. My mom calmly asked us to call our dad, who was at work, so he could take her to the hospital. Without hesitation, my dad rushed home, loaded all three of us into the Suburban, and took off down the hill toward the hospital.

The good news is my mom was fine, praise the Lord. Her elbow freed up with a minor procedure, and all was right again with the world. But that's not the point of this story. This was one of the first times I truly witnessed my dad under pressure. My mom's major surgeries and near-death experiences happened before my brother and I were adopted, so this was a new and scary experience for us.

Seeing how my dad reacted under pressure, how he responded to his wife's needs while simultaneously taking care of his rambunctious kids, left me speechless. There was a steadiness about him, even amid the hustle of the emergency room. There was a peace about him, even when his wife was in pain. There was a level-headedness about him, even when a million doctors bombarded him with information. His calm strength comforted my brother and me when we were worried about our mom. My dad was already my hero—he had been for a long time. But this instance only solidified that fact in my heart.

Another moment that stands out happened not long ago. Just a few days after God spoke to me in my biology lecture, saying, *Tara, you're not supposed to be here*, I told my parents I was thinking about leaving college. Not long after that, my dad met me for lunch at his request to talk about what was going on. We ordered our food, engaged in some small talk, and then it was time to get down to business.

My dad admitted that he was surprised. I mean, I don't blame him. More so than anyone else, my parents knew "the plan." I would go to college, get my degree, and become a medical practitioner. So when I announced that God had told me to leave everything good that I had going, my dad was thrown for a loop.

In between each bite of french fry, as I explained what God had been stirring in my heart, I became increasingly nervous. I feared what my dad was thinking. Would he tell me to suck it up, go back to school, and forget this ever happened? Would he tell me that he was disappointed in me?

My dad took a long sip of his Coke. He paused, carefully thinking through what he was going to say. What he said next about knocked me out of my chair.

"Tara, here's how your mother and I see it. Whatever path you choose, as long as you're following what God wants you to do, then that's all we could ask for."

In other words, he reminded me of a timeless truth from the heart of God. It doesn't necessarily matter *what* we do in this life as far as our occupation. What really matters is *who* we are following. *Who* we are obeying. If God says to work at a fast-food restaurant, then work at a fast-food restaurant. If God says go to medical school, then go to medical school. Any station of life and any occupation, done out of obedience to the Father, has the ability to glorify Him and fulfill His purposes for your life (1 Corinthians 10:31).

My dad grabbed my hand as my shoulders relaxed and jaw unclenched in relief. He proceeded to challenge me, however, and asked that I return to school and give it another week. Not necessarily to get another week of biology classes under my belt, but to saturate that time in prayer. In the presence of God. In communion with Him, so that I could be sure that it was, without a doubt, God's leading. Part of me hated that challenge, but the other part of me deeply admired it. Why? Because my dad had just poured out heavenly wisdom and discernment on my life.

What stood out to me from that encounter wasn't what restaurant we were at or what we had ordered from the menu. What stood out to me was my dad's character. The supernatural wisdom he exuded when he was very obviously caught off guard. Yet again, I got a front-row seat to see my dad's admirable character and the way he honored God in one of life's raw moments.

Know God, Love God, and Live for God

As fun as it would be to continue reminiscing and tell you some more of my favorite memories with my dad (some embarrassing, some hilarious), I promise there's a point to all of this.

I want you to think about the three people in your life who are closest to you. Think of your parents, spouse, best friend, boyfriend, grandmother, or mentor. What is something they all have in common (besides the fact that they all love you and think you're pretty great)?

May I venture a guess? The most obvious thing all those people have in common, no matter how random they may be, is that they *know* you. Not just the surface-level details. They know you at a deep, intimate level, and you know them in the same way. That's why they are important to you. You've seen each other in different seasons of life—the good, the bad, and the ugly. Over time you have gotten to know their true character and heart. And because you truly know who they are, you most likely trust them. You might even feel confident enough in your relationship with them to share your deepest secrets, hopes, and dreams.

When I look at my own life, I notice a pattern. The more I truly know someone, the more confident I am in trusting them. The more readily I want to share my secrets and struggles. The more I love them. For example, I don't have to question whether to trust Michael because I have gotten to know who he is over the last seven years. He's proven to me that he is an upright man of God. I have seen it firsthand.

The same goes for our relationship with God but on an even grander scale. If you've ever had a coffee conversation with me in person, tuned into any of my podcast episodes, or read any of my writing online, you've heard me say this phrase: "The more we know God, the more we'll love God, and the more we love God, the more we'll live for Him." It's become a slogan for my life and the ministry God has called me to.

It is, hands down, one of the greatest things God has taught me about Himself over the course of my life with Him. Living for God is the natural overflow of growing in our knowledge of and love for Him. And it makes sense, right?

We can't possibly *love* someone if we don't know them.

We can't possibly *trust* someone if we don't know them.

We can't possibly *want to do life* with them if we don't know them.

I suspect that a lot of us have gone through seasons of seeing God as someone who merely exists up there in the clouds. At various times in my life, God has felt far removed. He has felt unknown and ominous. As a little girl, I would read stories about God's character or listen to my parents or other people at our church talk about God in a personal way—how He was loving, kind, and trustworthy—but it was a long time before those realities struck a chord for me. These people didn't see God as a far-off, impersonal being. They saw His heart. His character. They really *knew* Him. They really *loved* Him. They really *trusted* Him.

I would always nod along in agreement, but honestly, I didn't get it. That confusion left me longing for what the Christians around me seemed to have: a deep and intimate knowledge of *who* God is. You've heard it said before: "Christianity isn't religion, it's relationship." Any healthy relationship (heavy emphasis on the *healthy*) in your life goes beyond the surface. Any relationship that is worthwhile, meaningful, or life-changing starts with knowing someone for who they truly are.

> THE MORE WE KNOW GOD, THE MORE WE'LL LOVE GOD, AND THE MORE WE LOVE GOD, THE MORE WE'LL LIVE FOR HIM.

I must tell you something amazing. Something shifted inside of me when I stopped settling for my surface-level knowledge of God. Something shifted inside of me when I started to question whether God was really this far-off figure, only existing in the clouds. And let me tell you, that shift was life-changing.

147

Moving from surface-level, secondhand knowledge about God to a deep, firsthand relationship with Him is a journey that's going to look a bit different for everyone. But as in any relationship, putting in the time and effort is the crucial foundation for developing real intimacy. Eventually, I decided I wanted to stop settling for anything other than a real relationship with the God and Savior I had given my life to.

Yes, this process starts with a desire to want more of God. It starts with an active, personal decision that only you can make—not one your parents, friends, spouse, or I can make for you. But from that decision point, it is a *process*, a *practice*, and a *progression* that we take on with our eyes fixed above (Colossians 3:2).

In its earliest stages this looked like taking daily Bible time with the Lord more seriously and planning my days around it, rather than planning Bible time around my days. I started praying more seriously, asking God to help me *want* to spend time in the Word and *want* to truly know Him. I started to get involved in church functions and fellowship groups to find community, accountability, and the benefit of being "built up" by the church (1 Thessalonians 5:11).

Remember that starting is often imperfect. Sometimes, along the way, you make great progress, and then one day you seem to take a few steps back. What's important about beginning your journey to truly knowing God is to get back on track when you have wondered off the path. What's important is to lay your soul bare to the Lord daily, displaying your desire to go deeper with Him and acknowledging your need for help. God is faithful. He is just aching to show you who He truly is and the beauty that comes when you don't give up in your pursuit of knowing Him.

Because the more you get to know God, the deeper you will fall in love with Him. The more willing you will be to trust His promises and obey His good commands. The more excited you will be to read

His Word and desire it every day. The easier and more joyful it will become to release your control and surrender to Him instead.

If you're worn and weary, tired of merely limping through life with a shallow knowledge of God, if you're ready to go deeper in your relationship with God, if you're committed to truly releasing your death grip on control and surrendering your story to God instead—stay with me.

Realistically, we could spend a whole lifetime talking about the character traits and qualities of God. But for the sake of our time together, I'm inviting you to study just a few of my favorite attributes of God.

If you walk away with anything from this chapter, I hope it is a deeper excitement and love for the God you have given your life to. I hope this sparks curiosity, longing, and excitement to continue on your journey of getting to know God. Why? Because anyone who truly knows God cannot help but love Him. And out of that overflow of love comes a deep trust, which enables you to surrender to God because you know—really and truly *know* in your heart—that God is writing a better story for your life than you ever could.

Getting to Know God

We could spend an entire lifetime studying the characteristics of God and still never scratch the surface. Here, though, are a few that have stood out the most in my life and along my journey of surrender.

GOD IS NEVER CHANGING

The world around us is in constant flux. It's always changing. The possibilities for modifying our lives are endless: whether that's something like changing up our hair color, our weight, our occupation, or even our day-to-day schedule. Governmental structures change. Family dynamics change. Occupations and finances change. That's just the way of the world.

But unlike us and the world we live in, our God never changes. Essential to His character is the fact that He remains the same. You may be thinking, *That sounds awfully boring.* Even though I'm not the biggest fan of change, I must admit that my life would feel somewhat stale without some sort of change—like the balayage color I tried on my hair or the new clothes I add to refresh my wardrobe.

But hear me out. The fact that God never changes is good news for us. When we say that God is immutable, or never changing, it means that *who He is* never changes. What He does—meaning His plans—never changes. What He promises never changes. His attributes and characteristics have been the same since before the world began, and they will continue to be the same through eternity. God never gets better or worse with time or experience.

Now, how is this good news? This may just sound as if God is outdated and stale. That He couldn't possibly keep up with the trends of the world or our ever-changing lives. But here's what is so comforting about the unchanging character of God: because God is unchanging, He is dependable.

Have you ever lied or broken a promise? As humans, we have the tendency to break our promises and go back on our word. You may have experienced this firsthand, dealing with people you cannot count on consistently. So the fact that God is never changing is wonderful news. Our trust in Him—unlike trust in ourselves, the world, or other people—can be a confident trust, knowing that His promises to us are unfailing, and His plans for our lives are reliable.

The God who created the earth at the dawn of time is the same God today. The God who was faithful to Israel and rescued them from slavery is the same God today. The God who enacted the greatest rescue mission to save humanity through His only begotten Son is the same God today. If He did it then, He will do it again.

THE WORLD WILL EBB AND FLOW. BUT GOD NEVER DOES. HIS PROMISES IN HIS WORD NEVER WILL.

Because God remains the same, we have a firm foundation to place our lives upon. Everything else is sinking sand. The world will ebb and flow. Our bodies will flux and change. Our careers and financial situations will change. But God never does. His promises in His Word never will. His plans for our lives and His glory will always be accomplished.

Verses to study: Psalm 90:2, Isaiah 40:8, Hebrews 13:8, Revelation 22:13

GOD IS SELF-SUFFICIENT

A few chapters back, we came face-to-face with the sobering reality that we were not created to be independent from God. We were not created to run our lives separate from Him. There may be times when we're tempted to believe we can do it all by ourselves, but that feeling goes against our God-given DNA.

However, on the flip side, God *is* self-sufficient. John 5:26 says, "For as the Father has life in himself, so he has granted the Son also to have life in himself." This verse is smack-dab in the middle of Jesus' conversation with an unbelieving crowd. He told them He had the power to raise people from the dead because, just like His heavenly Father, He had life in Himself.

It's no secret that we are needy people. We may not want to admit it, but we are. In stark contrast God has never once been in need of anything. His tank is utterly and completely full. He has no limitations or shortcomings. He has never once asked for help, and He never will.

This quality of God, the reality that He is self-sufficient, should bring supernatural peace and comfort to us. The fact that God has no needs and is entirely capable on His own should bring us to a place of awe and wonder. We serve a God who does not have deficiencies. We serve a God who does not need to rely on us—and that's a good thing, because Lord knows, we would let Him down.

Dear friend, let's not skip over this. When we know that God is self-sufficient, when we know that is just who He is, we are enabled and equipped to trust Him more with our lives. His self-sufficiency tells us that He is in control. All power, every resource, and every ability are at His fingertips. We don't have to worry about manipulating our timelines, rearranging our stories, or stressing over our plans when we have given our lives to a self-sufficient Savior.

———

Verses to study: John 5:26, John 15:5, 2 Corinthians 3:5

GOD IS OMNIPOTENT

Omnipotent is just a fancy-sounding way of saying that God is all powerful. It comes from Latin: *omni* = "all," and *potens* = "powerful."[8] When we hear the word *powerful*, it's usually used to describe something like someone's position in government, or the horsepower of one's car. But God has *all* the power and strength and might. Not just *some* power. He is the *definition* of power.

Omnipotence is who God is. It's an essential quality, woven deeply into the fabric of His divinity. When I'm at the gym and have a goal to lift heavier than I did last time, I need all the strength and power I can muster. But with God, it's another story. He doesn't have to muster up more power or strength deep within Himself to accomplish anything. It's effortless and natural because it's *who* He is.

God's omnipotence means He can do everything and anything He desires. It stands to reason that if God is all powerful, then whatever He plans to do will happen. There's nothing beyond God's reach or capabilities. How comforting is that? Nothing can stop what He has promised. Nothing—no government leader, natural disaster, pandemic, or circumstance—can turn back what He has set in motion.

It's no secret that the world has been crazy—not only over these last few years but really ever since the beginning of human history. But the reality that God is omnipotent should bring us great peace, confidence, and security. Believing God is all powerful—that nothing is beyond Him or too big for Him— empowers us to trust God more. Understanding the magnitude of His power helps us release our ideas about what we thought our lives would look like and instead surrender to His divine plan. Unlike some religions that worship a statue made of wood that can rot and decay, we live for a King who is all powerful and mighty. We live for a King who is the definition of power. And He's not one to abuse that power but always uses it for His glory and our good.

Verses to study: Job 42:1–2, Psalm 20:7, Psalm 147:5, Isaiah 14:27, Jeremiah 32:27, Luke 1:37, Hebrews 1:3–4

GOD IS OMNISCIENT

Put *omni* = "all" and *scire* = "knowledge" together and what do you get? "All knowing."[9] God isn't just smart and knowledgeable by our human standards. He *is* knowledge. God makes the IQ test look like child's play.

Have you ever been called a know-it-all? That's a name that usually carries negative connotations. But if someone were to call God a know-it-all, they wouldn't be wrong.

Omniscience is unique to God alone. He knows how many hairs are on your head. He knows how many grains of sand there are on the entire earth. He knows what thoughts will pop up in your head, always. He knows what jobs and roles you will occupy in your life. He knows when you will enter this world and when you will exit this world. The list goes on.

As we discussed with God's omnipotence, His omniscience means we can trust Him. Because God knows all our steps, we are free to humble ourselves and admit we don't know it all. But what a blessing that God does! We can celebrate the fact that we are in relationship with an all knowing God, one who doesn't leave us in the dark but gives us all we need for life and godliness (2 Peter 1:3). When we meditate on this attribute of God, it makes it easier to trust Him with everything going on in our lives—from the silliest delights to the most serious questions and heartaches.

Verses to study: Psalm 147:5, Isaiah 46:9–10, Isaiah 55:8–9, Romans 11:33–36, 1 John 3:20

GOD IS FAITHFUL

It would be completely off-brand of me not to give a shout-out to my online best friend, Thesaurus.com. As I contemplated God's faithfulness, I decided to see what synonyms came up for the word *faithful*. Some of my favorites were *loyal*, *steadfast*, and *constant*.

"The faithfulness of God" is not a new phrase to you or me. We've most likely heard it mentioned by our pastor on a Sunday morning, read it in an Instagram caption from our favorite influencer, or seen it on a farmhouse sign at Hobby Lobby. We may even thank God in our prayers for His faithfulness. But what does it really mean?

Faithfulness is His constancy and steadfastness as He relates to His people. For example, in the Old Testament, we see God's faithfulness in the way He never deserted Israel. Although they rebelled, disobeyed, and even went after small *g* gods, God remained faithful to them. He never forsook them. He remained constant and steady. For God to be faithful meant He never broke a promise and never went back on His word.

The apostle Paul praised God's faithfulness over and over in the Epistles, recalling how God was faithful to keep His promise about a Messiah who would save the world. In the book of Esther the Lord demonstrated His constancy and steadfastness to Esther and the Jews, even amid threat of a genocide. Although Simon Peter repeatedly denied Jesus as the Christ, Jesus stayed true to His word about how He would use Peter to build the church. We can read an incredible summary of God's faithfulness throughout the Old Testament by the first martyr of the early church, Stephen, in Acts 7.

When someone says they are faithful to their spouse, it means they are committed to the other, no matter the circumstances, regardless of life's ups and downs or the ways they (or their circumstances) may change. This is true about the Lord's faithfulness, but on an even greater scale! In fact, Scripture often describes God's faithfulness in terms of a marriage covenant.

As with any attribute of God, it's more than a quality He possesses. He *is* faithful. You could even say that He is faithfulness itself. He can't help but display it in His relationship with you, me, and the rest of humankind, because God is always nothing more or less than Himself—and He is faithful.

When we know God is faithful, it empowers us to trust Him more. When we trust that He always keeps His promises and that He never abandons His people, it empowers us to abide even deeper in the True Vine (John 15). Doesn't it bring you comfort knowing God is constant and steadfast? Doesn't it give you peace and security knowing God keeps His promises? That since He kept His promise to send a Savior and ransom you from death, He is worth trusting with the rest of your days?

The fact that God is faithful inspires me to be faithful right back to Him. To be steadfast, obedient, and committed to following Him. To be obedient when God says, *Dear child, release control and trust Me. Take up your cross and follow Me.*

Verses to study: Deuteronomy 7:9, 1 Corinthians 1:9, 2 Timothy 2:13, Hebrews 10:23

GOD IS GOOD

This is a hard but essential lesson, and it's something all of us have faced: my definition of *good* and God's definition of *good* are oftentimes very different. Take Romans 8:28 for example: "And we know that for those who love God, *all things work together for good*, for those who are called according to his purpose" (emphasis added). Our first instinct is to define *good* in our terms—like increased wealth, stellar health, a large social media following, or an engagement ring.

But God has a different definition for the word *good*. He *is* good and He *does* good. We can shout "God is good" all day but not really understand what that means. So let's dig a little deeper. An easy way to describe this character trait is to say that God has no evil in Him, that His intentions and motivations are always pure, and that He always does what is right for His people and His purposes.

Everything God created is good. His laws and commandments and everything He has said are good. They are upright, just, and completely fair. And ultimately, the greatest example of His goodness is seen through His redemption of the world from sin. In God's goodness He sent Jesus to become the perfect sacrifice. But here's the kicker: Because God is wholly good, He must judge sin. He can have no part of it. That's where Jesus enters—the forgiver of sins. The One who canceled our debt and made us pure in God's eyes.

When we know God is good—that He is pure in all of His intentions, loving in all of His decisions, and never sins—we are freed up to trust Him more. We don't have to question whether God's purposes and intentions are coming from a genuine place. We don't have to wonder if God is out to get us or tempt us. God is good and does only good things. He creates only good plans. He cannot possibly have any part in evil. So we don't have to worry about His intentions, His plans, or His purposes. We can trust Him more because there is no evil in Him. He is good to His core, and He is good to His people.

———

Verses to study: Psalm 34:8, Psalm 145:9, John 3:16

GOD IS LOVING

Nothing says it better than Scripture: not only does God love us, He *is* love (1 John 4:16). This love is an action expressed toward all of humanity, and it's also an attribute of His heart.

As self-sufficient as He is, God wants to show us love and wants our love in return. As easy as it would be for Him not to have any interaction with us, He actively chooses to pursue us in love. Our Savior does not *need* our love. Our Savior does not need to show us love. And yet He *wants* to show us His heart, which is full and overflowing with love.

When you love someone, and I mean *truly* love someone, that love is usually accompanied by action, proof, or evidence. In the same way, God's love is active, not passive. Whether we believe it or not, God's love is always for the betterment of His people and the advancement of His kingdom. Every plan, purpose, and decision God executes is out of love. How is this possible? Well, because God *is* love, every move and decision He makes comes from a place of love.

Do you realize that God loves us regardless of anything we've done? That His love isn't based on our living up to certain requirements? Because God is love, we can breathe easier. We can unclench our fists and surrender. Practically, we can retrain our minds to see God as loving and not withholding. When we insist on our own way and grasp for personal control instead of surrendering to God, we subconsciously believe the lie that God does not care enough about us to write good stories for our lives; perhaps He's "holding out on us." That is why this quality of God is so important. God can never do anything that isn't backed by love—for His glory and our good. Even if life doesn't go our way, we can rest knowing that God loves us too much to give us anything less than His best.

Verses to study: Psalm 86:15, Isaiah 54:10, Romans 5:8, 1 John 4:7–10

Taste and See that He Is Good

You know, I could spend all day talking about the characteristics of our heavenly Father. I could have dedicated more space to His qualities in this chapter. Lord knows, I didn't even scratch the surface!

But as I mentioned before, none of us can have a *true* relationship with the Lord that is purely based on secondhand knowledge. None of us can experience true life in Christ without knowing Christ Himself. Like my parents have always told my brother and me, "You have to make your faith your own."

King David said it like this: "Oh, taste and see that the LORD is good!" (Psalm 34:8). The verb *taste* in this context is a metaphor for personal experience. That is exactly what a relationship with Christ is meant to be: personal and intimate. Something experienced up close and personal, not lived vicariously through your parents, spouse, or favorite Instagram influencer.

How can we possibly release our death grip on control, surrender our stories, and trust someone we do not know? How can we possibly pick up our crosses and enter into the unknown with someone we're not truly, deeply, and intimately acquainted with? How can we wholeheartedly believe that God is good, loving, all powerful, and all of the other qualities we've talked about if we have not tasted? If we have not seen? If we have not really known?

I promise you, dear friend:

The more you know God, the deeper you will fall in love
    with Him.
The more you know God, the more you will be able to
    trust Him.

The more you know God, the more excited you will be to read His Word and follow Him.

The more you know God, the more willing you will be to release your control and surrender.

He's just that good. It's time to taste and see.

Space to Surrender

Grow in the grace and knowledge of our Lord and Savior Jesus Christ.

2 PETER 3:18

1. Did any of the things you learned about God in this chapter change how you think about Him? How so? Is there a characteristic about God in particular that encourages you the most?

2. Trusting someone enough to surrender your own hopes and plans to them is pretty much impossible unless you have a deep, intimate relationship. How would you describe your relationship with God right now?

3. In his *Confessions*, Augustine said that God is "closer to me than I am to myself." In other words no one knows, understands, or loves you more intimately than the God who created you. Try making a habit of meditating on the nearness of God—it's a great way to build your trust

in Him! Write down some other characteristics of God that we didn't mention in this chapter that encourage your heart to praise Him.

Lord, thank You that You are so good, all powerful, and all knowing. I want to get to know You personally and intimately. I pray that You would help me to make time to be with You in Your Word. I want to know You more, love You more, and in turn, trust You more with my story.

CHAPTER 9

Standing on the Promises of God

If Jesus is the Son of God, his teachings
are more than just good ideas from a
wise teacher; they are divine insights on
which I can confidently build my life.
LEE STROBEL

GROWING UP AS PART-TIME FARM kids, my brother and I
loved to take advantage of every opportunity to zip around the
farm on our minibikes, ATVs (all-terrain vehicles, aka four-
wheelers) and UTVs (utility task vehicles, which are kind of like

ATVs but have a cab and a steering wheel). From a young age, our parents taught us how to (safely) ride and operate ATVs. After some training and adult supervision, riding these machines became second nature for us—shifting up and down, bearing down on the throttle, and doing cookies (or donuts, depending on where you're from) in the fields. The main reason my dad and his brothers bought these fun machines wasn't for joyrides but for work. They were used every day for tasks like pulling a trailer hauling hazelnut trees to and from location or driving through a field as you pruned. But when my brother and I were little, all we saw was the chance to play.

The first four-wheeler I learned to drive was a manual, meaning you couldn't just push a button and go. You had to manually shift up or down with your foot to tell it what to do. I listened intently as my dad explained each gear. He went down the list: park, neutral, first, second, and, finally, third gear. The three numbered gears and park were relatively self-explanatory in my mind. Park was the gear you would shift into when you were done riding and ready to turn the key to off. First was the slowest, second was right in the middle, and third was the speediest for this old vehicle. Guess which gear my brother and I loved to race in?

But neutral was the gear that didn't make a lot of sense to me. What was the purpose? If you were on any sort of slight incline or hill and you shifted into neutral, you would start to roll down the hill. If you were on a flat surface and you shifted into neutral, you would just sit there. If you wanted to use the throttle or stomp on the brakes, nothing would happen. It was as if your four-wheeler was incapacitated. Paralyzed. Helpless. You can probably guess that I rarely used that gear, and you would be correct.

The ironic thing is that although I considered neutral to be the absolute silliest and most useless gear on an ATV, I grew up living most of my life in a similar pattern. From the outside looking in, you probably wouldn't have noticed it. I went to church. I was kind and warm to friends, family, and strangers alike. I owned a few Bibles and always had them on my nightstand. I bowed my head in prayer at each meal with my family. I did the Christian thing.

But inside I was disinterested and detached. Instead of putting action to my faith and relationship with God, I was coasting in neutral. Instead of living life out of first, second, or even third gear, it was easier to kick back in neutral and remain stationary. It really wasn't until I was diagnosed with fibromyalgia that I realized how messed up that was. I finally acknowledged how impersonal my relationship with God had been—and how unfulfilled and empty my life was as a result.

You see, I fully believe I had a genuine relationship with the Lord from the time I confessed Him as my Savior at a young age. There's no doubt in my mind. But instead of taking up my cross, denying myself, and following God—all extremely active aspects of the Christian life—I pushed my cross off to the side, did whatever I wanted, and followed God only when I felt like it.

Over the years, I have spent a lot of time questioning why.

Why was I so indifferent?
Why was I so numb?
Why was my life not bearing much fruit?
Why did I not care about what God had to say?

There are probably a lot of little reasons why I was so content with life in neutral, so stagnant and unaware, but there is one big reason I just can't ignore. One that I'm absolutely convinced was the main culprit.

The main reason why I felt so indifferent to God and had become so apathetic toward my faith was because my Bible sat on my nightstand for no other reason than to make me look holy. It wasn't something I feasted on and read daily, but something that helped fill space and decorate my nightstand.

What was missing from my life was God's Word. What fell through the cracks was an understanding of what makes God's Word so life-changing and powerful. Essentially, I was wandering around my life without a guide. Without a road map. Without something to teach me how to live for the Savior I claimed to love and devote my life to.

I'm sure we all have been told at one time or another not to let our Bibles accumulate dust. It sounds cute and trendy—a quote you would re-pin on Pinterest for all your friends to see, right? But for me, the dust on my Bible was *real*. I even remember picking it up for church one Sunday morning and finding that it had accumulated so much dust and random debris that it was partially stuck to my nightstand. I cringed as I peeled it away from the surface and headed out the door. Yikes. Talk about embarrassing.

Now, I want you to hear me loud and clear when I say this: reading the Bible still doesn't always come naturally to me. I'm a flawed human. I'm distracted often. I make excuses and put things above God and time with Him in the Word. This isn't going to be a chapter where I tell you how perfect I am or how easy it was to make this shift from a dusty Bible to a well-loved and well-read Bible.

Perhaps you found yourself nodding along in agreement as I shared my story about my dusty Bible. Perhaps, whether it was easy to admit or not, you found yourself relating to my feelings of indifference and laziness when it came to reading God's Word.

If you did, I'm here to tell you that you're not alone, and you're not a horrible person.

But if we want to truly release our death grip on control, surrender our stories, and trust God instead, we need to dust off our Bibles. If we want a better way to live, if we want a road map for our lives that doesn't leave us constantly frustrated after our plans have fallen apart, it's time to start reading.

Just as the human body needs the heart to survive, so the Christian needs the Bible. Just as the trees and plants of the earth need oxygen to grow, so the Christian needs the Bible. Just as we need GPS directions to get to a new location, so the Christian needs the Bible.

> JUST AS WE NEED GPS DIRECTIONS TO GET TO A NEW LOCATION, SO THE CHRISTIAN NEEDS THE BIBLE.

How could we possibly surrender our stories if we do not know what God's Word says? How could we possibly trust God and follow Him, even into the unknown, if we do not have a guide to follow day by day?

Friend, this chapter is for you if

- you are interested in knowing the Bible better,
- you want to read the Bible not just to check off some legalistic to-do list but to know God more deeply,
- you want to understand, interpret, and apply God's Word as it was intended and not be confused or bored anymore, or
- you are desperate for the Bible not just to go in one ear and out the other but to truly transform your life, help you to surrender your story, and trust God.

You Don't Need a PhD

Picture this. It's early in the morning and you are sitting down with your first cup of coffee of the day. Your couch, desk, or favorite cozy spot is covered with the essentials: your Bible, an adorable notebook, pens, and a handful of no-bleed highlighters in the prettiest pastel palette. The house is quiet, and you are in no hurry to get up and go anywhere.

You indulge in the last few sips of your delicious coffee and then set it aside as you pick up your Bible. A few moments go by as you flip through its pages and then, finally, you choose a passage to read that morning. But as you begin reading, something unexpected starts to happen. You begin to realize that none of what you're reading makes sense. The excitement you had when you sat down with your pile of supplies starts to slowly fade as God's words start to blur.

> "Who is this *Melchizedek* guy? Why do all these characters
> have such weird names?"
> "What does this outdated law have to do with anything?"
> "What does *that* word mean?"

Has this ever happened to you?

I can't tell you how many times I've opened God's Word, started to read, then all of a sudden realized that I was lost—that what I was reading didn't make sense to me. And because I had no idea what was going on in those pages, all I felt when I looked at my Bible was frustration. It was easier to shut the Bible than it was to keep on. As you may guess, that frustration ended up robbing me of the joy and excitement I should have had about spending time with God in His Word. I knew in my heart I should read the Bible, but it was starting to feel like an overwhelming and unbeatable task.

It was starting to feel like God's Word was something only the pastors at my church could understand, or those with PhDs, the famous scholars who have come before, or maybe even the Christian influencers who have a lot of followers.

There's an enemy prowling around this world. He's out to kill, steal, and destroy, and he does this through deception and discouragement. Through lies and feelings of hopelessness. When he looks at God's children, he sees opportunity after opportunity to strike.

Remember how Satan conned Eve and convinced her to do a double take on God's instructions? Through his lies, Satan called into question God's character and God's word, and Eve believed it. In its own way, that happens to you and me today. We open our Bibles and find ourselves confused about what we just read. We want to understand it and experience the incredible life transformation we know it holds. But the Enemy begins to whisper lies into our hearts and minds: *You're not smart enough to understand what God is saying. You haven't gone to the right school or been a Christian that long. There's no way you could ever get this. It's so far beyond you, so why try?*

But there is good news that shatters these lies into millions of tiny pieces. There is good news that eases our insecurities, our feelings of inadequacy, or fears when it comes to reading the Bible.

If you are in Christ, if you have given your life to Him, then His Word is for you. His Word is accessible to you. His Word can absolutely, 100 percent, beyond a shadow of a doubt, be understood by you through His empowerment. His Word has the power to change your life (yes, your very own life). His Word is not hidden from you, and it holds nothing back from you.

Read Deuteronomy 30:11–14 with me: "For this command-ment that I command you today *is not too hard for you, neither is it far off.* It is not in heaven, that you should say, 'Who will ascend to heaven for us and bring it to us, that we may hear it and do it?' Neither is it beyond the sea, that you should say, 'Who will go over the sea for us and bring it to us, that we may hear it and do it?' *But the word is very near you. It is in your mouth and in your heart, so that you can do it*" (emphasis added).

Now, Moses, the author of the book of Deuteronomy, was talking specifically about the laws and commandments God had given to the people of Israel. But the principle applies to all of Scripture and to all people who follow God. Notice first what Moses does *not* say here.

X   He does not say that God's Word is not too hard for them to understand and obey because they were God's chosen people or went to four years of seminary.

X   He does not say that they have the ability to understand God's Word because they're a smarter, "more elite" society.

✓   What Moses *does* say is that the Bible is not too hard, too far off, or too complicated for them to understand. Why? Because if they put their faith in God and find true salvation through His covenant, they can understand and obey God's Word for themselves.

This promise is one that you and I can also claim today. Whether we feel smart enough or equipped enough, if we are in Christ, the amazing, unchangeable truth is that God's Word is for us. It's not hidden from us. God wants us to know Him. He desperately aches for His children to immerse themselves head-first into His Word, understand it, and never come back to the surface.

He's a Man of His Word

One of my favorite worship songs is "Man of Your Word" by Maverick City Music. Spotify must know I am obsessed with it because it plays multiple times a day. A lyric they repeat in the song goes like this: "If You said it, we believe it. You're a man of Your word."[10]

When I sing it, whether that be in the car or in my bathroom while doing my makeup, the repetition of those lines challenges me to preach this truth over my soul—reminding me that God is in fact a man of His word. God, in fact, keeps His promises.

R. C. Sproul once said, "We break our promises to one another. We break our promises to God. But God never breaks His promises to us."[11]

Our heavenly Father operates in guarantees and vows because, simply put—that is who He is. That is an essential part of His character, namely, his faithfulness (just as we learned in the last chapter). But God's promises are very different from ours. When I think of promises from a worldly standpoint, I think about the times I've promised my husband that I would clean out the lint tray of our dryer after each laundry load. Needless to say, I have broken that promise many times and he still reminds me. (Although I'm getting better, right, honey?) When we promise to do (or stop doing) something, it often means we'll do our best to remember, but let's be honest, our follow-through is going to be very hit-or-miss.

But God's promises are on a completely different scale. His promises in His Word are not flippant maybes. They are commitments. All His promise are yes and amen.

Rock Versus Sand

I'm sure you've heard the Bible described as God's love letter to His children. Although I agree, I'd love to suggest another name for God's Word.

God's book of promises.

The Bible isn't just a book of love stories to a people He died for, but a book of promises to His children *because* of His love. From Genesis to Revelation, we read the story of a God who so loved the world that He made a promise to it—to send His one and only Son. Within that overarching promise of salvation, God also wrote countless promises that changed the lives of those in the Old Testament and New Testament, and they still ring true for you and me today.

Sometimes, the Enemy convinces me that God's promises aren't true because of how I'm feeling. Because of the circumstances of my life. Because of the pain, suffering, and injustice of the world. We face challenges every single day that tempt us to believe God can't be taken at His word: physical pain, frustration, broken plans, crushed dreams, relationship drama, lies from the Enemy, and more.

But that's where faith over feelings comes into play. Consider:

- "We destroy arguments and every lofty opinion raised against the knowledge of God, and take every thought captive to obey Christ." (2 Corinthians 10:5)

- "Do not be conformed to this world, but be transformed by the renewal of your mind, that by testing you may discern what is the will of God, what is good and acceptable and perfect." (Romans 12:2)

Scripture commands us to take our thoughts captive—to not allow our thoughts to persuade us against God's truth but instead align them with God's Word. We're encouraged to renew our minds—taking what we think or what the world says and filtering it through Scripture. When our feelings, thoughts, or circumstances tell us to question God, our job is to stop, capture, and filter—because God's promises are true regardless of what we feel, see, or think. Like "Man of Your Word" boldly declares, if God said it, we *will* believe it. Even if we don't feel like it in the moment, something powerful happens when we choose to declare God's truth back to Him, training our hearts to believe His promises.

Jesus told a story of two builders in Matthew 7:24–27. One builder chose to build on the rock. When the rain, floods, and winds beat on the house and its foundation, the house did not fall because "it had been founded on the rock." The other builder chose to build on the sand. When the rain, floods, and winds beat on the house and its foundation, the house "fell, and great was the fall of it."

That right there, my friend, is why it is so important to build our lives on the solid Rock of Jesus Christ. That is why it is so important to build our lives on His Word and nothing else. The religious leaders of Jesus' time had foolishly believed they could build their lives upon self-righteousness. They were trying to build their lives on their own strength and the wisdom of this world. But Jesus asserted that a true disciple would be known by choosing a very different foundation—taking His words to heart and living by them.

If we drift from God's Word, our faith will dwindle. Our prayer life will wane. Our relationship with God will weaken. Our joy will diminish. Our hope will wither. Our ability to trust God and surrender our stories will fade.

Become a Better Reader

If you're reading this, you're likely hungry to know God more, love Him more, and learn how to surrender your story. Whether you've known God your whole life, just recently accepted Him as your Savior, or are somewhere in between, you have a desire to understand God's Word more. You want to move beyond merely checking off the "quiet time and Bible reading" box on your to-do list and really grow in your faith.

Therefore, we need to become better readers. But becoming a better Bible reader doesn't just happen. It helps to have a strategy, a few key steps that you can follow while reading God's Word. Beyond mere reading, we need to become *interpreters* and ultimately *doers* of God's Word so that we can build our lives on Christ, our foundation. When our habits have been shaped by Scripture, we'll be ready when life inevitably happens. When we're faced with an opportunity to attempt to take control and live in our own strength or wisdom, if we've been immersed in the Bible, our thoughts, perceptions, and habits will already be shaped toward trusting God instead.

If you're reading this book, then you obviously know how to read. But there's a difference between knowing how to read and being a good reader in Bible study. If we don't want to just skim the surface, but truly understand and see life transformation, we need to be more than just readers. We need to be biblical *detectives*.

KEEP YOUR BRAIN IN GEAR

They call it Bible "study" for a reason. I know what you're thinking: study usually makes us think of school, which could likely make many people bored. But I like to think of this in terms of keeping my brain in gear. An ATV left in neutral isn't much fun—but it's downright exhilarating when you start shifting through the gears and picking up speed!

Keeping your brain in gear while reading Scripture means reading actively, not passively. Instead of simply breezing through a chapter a day, prepare your mind to think deeply. Be ready to wrestle with challenging commands, linger over thought-provoking truths, and pursue answers to tough questions. Reading Scripture involves more than a glance or casual approach.

Keeping your brain in gear while reading Scripture also means not allowing your mind to be overtaken by distractions. Keeping your brain in gear requires intentionality and staying focused on Scripture, not on your phone or other alluring distractions. The life-changing truth of God is in the Bible. But we must go after it.

FOCUS ON CONSISTENCY AND REPETITION

We all know someone who has read the Bible from cover to cover multiple times. Have you ever heard someone (whether in real life or on social media) mention that they've just finished reading the whole Bible . . . again? I used to be irritated by those people, but as time has passed (and as God has softened my heart), I've started to long for that same accomplishment. Not to be performative or show off to my friends, but to say that I have hidden God's *entire* Word in my heart. And the best way to get God's Word in my heart is to read it often and repeatedly.

It never ceases to amaze me that God's Word was written thousands of years ago, and yet it remains true. It holds the same life-changing power and insights that it had in the beginning, and it will never stop. Unlike some books, the Bible will never go out of style. The layers of meaning and the depth of truth it contains ensure that we can still find new, amazing truths even in familiar passages we've read a hundred times.

Here are suggestions to help you create a discipline of reading the Bible every day:

- **No cherry-picking.** Read entire books of the Bible at a time, starting at the beginning. There are so many benefits to not skipping around the Bible and plucking out random verses. The value of reading entire books instead of cherry-picking is you'll see the overarching story of each book. Things remain in context. Think about it like this: when you sit down to watch a movie, you don't typically watch random snippets, skipping from one scene to another. You watch it from beginning to end. The same applies to the books of the Bible. Each individual book of the Bible—and how each book fits with the rest of Scripture—starts making sense when you prioritize context. My favorite method is to start at the first chapter, read one chapter a day, repeat until I've finished the book, and then move on to the next book of the Bible.

- **Change up your translation.** Reading the Bible in different translations keeps you from becoming overly familiar or bored with it. Different translations have different strengths, but I love challenging my brain to see familiar passages in a new light thanks to the way different translations approach the biblical languages. Try exploring some of my personal favorite translations: ESV, NASB, NLT, and CSB.

- **Try listening.** Read it out loud, get an audio Bible, or use an audio Bible app. Did you know that many generations of believers experienced the Scriptures primarily through hearing them read aloud? That alone is a great reason to give it a try. There's something about hearing the words read aloud that can make the concepts and ideas land on my heart in a new way. Plus, excuses that we're too busy to sit down and open our Bible fade away when we realize we could listen to an audio Bible while taking care of chores, driving to work, or running errands.

SLOW IT DOWN

There's value in reading through lots of Scripture content in quick succession. Some parts of the Bible, especially the stories, can be read quickly, moving from plot point to plot point. But that's not the only approach you should take. Focus on slowing down while you read. Be intentional about thoughtfully soaking up every word, every name mentioned, every promise given.

As you read, ask the obvious questions that we often forget:

Who? Who are the people/characters in the text? What is said about them? How are they described? What do they do?

What? What is happening in the text? What is the point or main message?

Where? Where is this taking place? Where is the writer? Why might the location be important?

When? Think about time. When do the events in this passage take place? When is the writer writing this? Sometimes the chronology provides additional context that helps us understand what's going on in the text and how to apply it to our lives today.

Why? Why was this passage included in Scripture? Why did the author include certain surprising details?

READ WITH A PRAYERFUL HEART

It's easy to think of Bible reading and prayer as two stand-alone things. However, they are vitally connected. Prayer serves so many purposes in our lives, but when it comes to Bible study, it is especially important when we

- don't have any desire or motivation to read God's Word but want to feel motivated or
- are stuck or confused by a passage and want to understand it.

Some simple ways to read prayerfully are to begin, continue, and end your Bible time with prayer. Begin by asking God to help you read, understand, and apply His truth as it's intended. If you get stuck, confused, or bored during your study, stop and ask the Spirit for His help. Pray when you close your Bible, and thank God for your special time with Him in the Word. Another way to read prayerfully is to turn Scripture into prayers, for example, using literal songs of praise and prayer from the Psalms as the basis for your own prayers to God.

From Confusion to Confidence

We all want to clear the fog when it comes to Bible reading, don't we? Interpreting and understanding Scripture is how we do that. The goal is to move from a place of confusion to clarity and from clarity to confidence. Understanding Scripture may be the biggest thing that we Christians struggle with when it comes to Bible study, but let me encourage you: God's Word is for us. God's Word isn't taunting us or playing an elusive game of hide-and-seek that we can never win. We can do this with God's help.

The world may say that truth is subjective and changeable, but that's not the case with God's Word. Here are some keys for understanding what the Bible is really saying. If we understand what it meant (what the author intended and how the original audience understood what they were reading or hearing), we'll be better equipped to understand what the Bible means for us today and how to apply it to our lives.

UNDERSTAND BIBLICAL GENRES

There's a big difference between a book about motherhood and breastfeeding and a book about United States history. Those books simply cannot be read or approached the same way because they aren't the same genre. The same goes for our approach to God's Word. Even though the Bible is a unified whole, there are many different genres or categories of books that make up the Bible.

Be on the lookout for genres like exposition, narratives, parables, poetry, wisdom literature, and prophecy. Without knowing the genre, there's a good chance you'll misunderstand something about what you're reading. For example, if you read a wisdom book like Proverbs, thinking it's a prophetic book, you will be sorely confused! One of my favorite books that has helped me define biblical genres is *Basic Bible Interpretation* by Roy B. Zuck.[12]

UNDERSTAND CONTEXT

It's said context is key, and I couldn't agree more. Prioritizing context helps us honor God's Word, understand it, and be better stewards of it in our own lives and as we teach others. To understand the context, look at each verse in the context of the chapter, and think about the chapter in the context of the entire book, as opposed to cherry-picking. Think of it as if you're a photographer using a telescopic, wide-angle lens instead of a narrow one. It's great to focus close-up on the detail, but there's also value in pulling back and literally seeing the big picture.

Here are a few kinds of context to be on the lookout for in your study:

- **Literary context.** Think of the words *before* and *after* when it comes to literary context. Consider and study the chapters, paragraphs, and sections before and after each verse. This helps you see the whole picture when you read a section in its entirety.

- **Historical context.** Many people muddle a passage's meaning because they don't consider when it was written or the situation of either the author or the intended audience. Many of the passages in the Bible aren't directly about us. For example, huge sections of the Old Testament are primarily about God's relationship with a particular nation or even a specific generation. These passages can be encouraging to us or provide us with important lessons, but before trying to decipher their meaning for us today, we need to have a clear sense of the original historical context. (A study Bible or commentary will be your best friend in this endeavor.)

- **Cultural and geographical context.** This goes hand in hand with historical context. Get to know the people—who they were, what their day-to-day lives looked like, and where they lived. Principles and concepts found in a passage of Scripture will make more sense when we know who it is being written to or spoken about. For example, it's important for us to know that Paul was writing to the church at Corinth in 1 and 2 Corinthians. One of the main messages we read about in 1 Corinthians has to do with sexual immorality. That focus makes sense given the fact that the people of Corinth at that time were especially exposed to the influence of pagan culture and idol worship, and as a result, they were struggling to live purely. Can you see why this is so important? Knowing the culture and day-to-day lives of biblical characters is key to unlocking your understanding of why the book was written.

- **Theological context.** This asks the question, "What did this author know about God?" We know that the Bible has not always been available to us as a finished copy, and here's why that matters: earlier generations weren't aware of later developments in God's relationship with His people. When you're reading about Abraham, it's important to remember that he lived before God gave Moses the law and before God's covenant with David. In fact, Abraham didn't have a Bible—the first books of the Bible weren't written until much later. Abraham's understanding of God was based on a close personal relationship, but while reading about Abraham it's useful for us to keep in mind that at that time God's revelation of Himself to humanity was in its very early stages. This is called "progressive revelation." Theological context reminds us to look at where humanity was in God's grand, redemptive story when a particular book was written.

Knowing It and Living It

Let's talk about application. It's often the most exciting part for us when we read an Instagram devotional or blog post, or listen to a sermon. It's exciting because it gives us something to do.

But here's the key: we can't properly apply God's Word or see true life transformation if we don't utilize the first two components we talked about—reading and interpreting. When we have become excellent readers of God's Word and understand God's Word in context (not just on the surface), then we can properly apply the truths and live them out rightly. Application is the culmination, the grand finale you could say, of all the steps.

James 1:22 challenges us to "be doers of the word, and not hearers only." If we are great readers and great interpreters but crummy appliers, then we've missed the point. God wants us not only to dig deep into the Bible's concepts but to be changed by them. To some that may sound scary. Change is uncomfortable. But the good news in Christ is that any change God has for us in His Word is *always* good for us. He loves us too much to let us stay the same. He desires us to be sanctified—to keep reaching new heights of glory. And that doesn't stop with you and your own heart. God's plan to change the world involves transforming individual hearts, and that adds up over time. When you read and apply God's Word, you're taking part in the much bigger story of God's redemptive purposes for the world.

The Transforming Power of God's Word

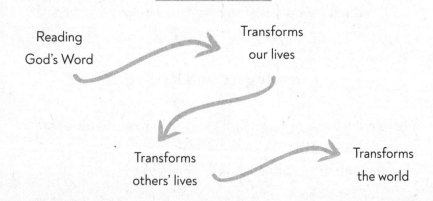

Reading God's Word

Transforms our lives

Transforms others' lives

Transforms the world

Think of applying Scripture in terms of these questions: How can we take what we just read and let it change who we are for the better? Are we convicted, convinced, and then changed?

Here are four possible steps for applying God's Word:

- **Know what you're reading.** Have firsthand, up-close-and-personal knowledge of what you're reading. We've learned that comes from being a better reader and interpreter. In the same vein, know yourself. Be realistic with your weaknesses, strengths, and sin. If we don't see our sin and the areas in which we need to grow, then we won't change. Ask God to reveal who you are, even if it's not pretty. He won't shame you for your sin. He knows you better than you know yourself and what He wants to do with that is make you even more like Him. What a win!

- **Compare.** I'm not saying to unhealthily compare yourself to other people, okay? What I mean by *compare* is to relate the truth of the Bible to ourselves, our lives, and our experiences. There is nothing in our lives, nothing we could think of, that God's Word does not give wisdom to. Obviously, we should keep context in mind and not apply things to ourselves that were only meant for a particular person or culture described in the Bible. But remember, the Bible is not some ambiguous, distant book that doesn't have power for our lives. Jesus Christ wants to renew every area of who we are with His Word. Make it personal.

- **Meditate.** God encourages us to let the truth of His Word take root in our lives, and meditation is a key strategy for making that happen. Now, some forms of meditation are not compatible with a Christian worldview. But for Christians, scriptural meditation means reflecting on, dwelling on, or contemplating what God's Word says. David told us to meditate on the law of the Lord day and night—weaving Scripture into the fabric of our everyday lives, saturating our every moment with what God's Word says. The more we meditate on Scripture the more it becomes part of who we are, enabling us to live according to God's wisdom rather than our own.

- **Practice, practice, practice.** Practice makes perfect—or in this case, practice aids in sanctification. The goal of reading our Bible is to be changed and transformed, which requires practicing and putting into action what we read. This looks like taking what we've read in the Bible and asking the Lord if there's an area in our lives that needs this truth. It's taking God's commands and instructions and obeying them. If obedience to His Word, especially the hard, countercultural things, sounds like an impossible task, let me tell you this: when you've cultivated a genuine love for God and desire for His Word, obedience will follow. I'm not saying it will be easy, but obedience flows from a heart that loves God and understands He only asks us to do things for our betterment and His glory.

THERE IS NOTHING IN OUR LIVES, NOTHING WE COULD THINK OF, THAT GOD'S WORD DOES NOT GIVE WISDOM TO.

Space to Surrender

Do not be conformed to this world, but be transformed by the renewal of your mind, that by testing you may discern what is the will of God, what is good and acceptable and perfect.

ROMANS 12:2

1. Name one or two obstacles you have when it comes to reading your Bible consistently, and challenge yourself to overcome them with the help of the Holy Spirit.

2. Find a passage of Scripture, whether random or one you are studying in your quiet time, and try to answer these questions about that particular passage, if applicable. This is an awesome exercise in being better "biblical detectives" and knowing God's Word more, which will ultimately help us grow in our trust of Him.

- Is there an example or command for me to follow?
- Is there a sin for me to avoid?
- Is there a promise of God for me to hold on to and take comfort in?
- Is there a challenge or hardship that I should be aware of so I can persevere?
- Is there a character trait of God that I should learn about?

Father, I believe Your promises are good and Your Word is true. Thank You for giving us the Bible as our guide; help me to follow it daily. Give me the confidence to be a good reader, interpreter, and applier of the Bible so that I can love You more and trust You deeper.

Ready, Set, Surrender

Take the first step in faith. You don't have to see
the whole staircase, just take the first step.
MARTIN LUTHER KING JR.

HERE'S A RANDOM FACT ABOUT me: I know *a lot* about hazelnuts. Yes—I'm talking about those little brown nuts that make up one of the world's most beloved, spreadable snacks, Nutella. (But they're so much more than that, as much as I love Nutella on a pretzel chip.) When you grow up on a hazelnut farm with a dad who is a third-generation farmer, it's inevitable.

When I was in elementary school, I learned how to plant my

very first hazelnut tree. My dad and his brothers not only harvest the hazelnuts in-shell but also plant and propagate the hazelnut tree seedlings to sell to other farmers so that they can plant budding fields of their own and make a profit. After the tiny seedlings grow in a tray among seventy or so of their siblings, we carefully transplant them to bigger plastic pots where they will grow up to six or seven feet before they are sold and put in the ground where they will grow for the rest of their lives.

To prepare the seedlings to be repotted, I was taught to carefully remove each tree from the tray, ensuring that its roots did not snap or break off. Next, we dug a decent-sized hole in the pot with our fingers. After the hole was created, we nestled the tree into the dirt and covered it up with the remaining dirt so that it would stand upright. After all of that was done, the trees were watered in their pots and placed in a warm greenhouse that was perfectly prepared for their needs. On a predetermined schedule they would be watered, fertilized, and weeded.

This process was usually repeated a few times a year, and then there would be thousands upon thousands of trees, ordered and purchased by excited farmers, ready to be planted in the ground. In what seemed like a blink of an eye, each root had skyrocketed in width, depth, and durability. Each trunk had grown thicker and stronger. Each leaf had expanded and deepened into a beautiful shade of green, creating the perfect sunshade both to protect the tree and soak up nutrients.

Writing this process out in words is much easier and faster than the actual process of growing a healthy hazelnut tree. What took just a couple of paragraphs to describe takes almost an entire calendar year (or more) of waiting, pruning, constant attention, care, and weeding. All so these trees will not only grow but flourish.

The same goes for surrendering our stories—releasing our death grip on control and trusting God instead. Like the hazelnut tree, growth in our lives and in this area does not happen overnight. It does not happen at the flick of a switch, as much as we wish it did. It takes discipline, dedication, and desire.

All that sounds like really hard work that might be boring, tedious, and tiresome. But it is the way to the abundant life that Jesus purchased for us on the cross, the new life which He literally died for, hoping we would choose to live for Him. As John 10:10–11 says, "The thief comes only to steal and kill and destroy. I came that they may have life and have it abundantly. I am the good shepherd. The good shepherd lays down his life for the sheep."

This promise from Jesus' heart in the Gospel of John is so important for us to hold on to and remember. Jesus spoke to the attentive crowd with a metaphor they would understand in their time, setting, and culture: farming. (Side note: pay attention to how often Jesus uses farming and agricultural metaphors in the Bible. Jesus loved the farmer, and that brings a great smile to my part-time, fourth-generation, farming heart.) In context Jesus was telling His audience that the only way to salvation is through Him. In the verses that follow, He promised abundant life and blessing to those who would take up their crosses, deny themselves, and follow Him. But Jesus, the Good Shepherd, also made it clear: the abundant life He offered would not be without its share of difficulties, but it would not be boring or miserable. The abundant life that only Jesus can give does not squash the dreams of His people or rid them of their unique personalities. The abundant life is intended to be rich, full, and joy-filled. The abundant life for those who follow Jesus well will overflow with meaning—not just in the here and now but into eternity.

To a people who were used to living under the Old Testament laws, often slipping into legalism and ritualism, this must have been groundbreaking. This must have been news to them. This must have felt upside-down. But as we saw earlier, Jesus came to bring an upside-down kingdom, a kingdom that's counterintuitive and surprising in the best of ways. He came to make clear what was unclear. He came to reveal what was hidden. He came to offer a solution to the challenges that come with being a true follower of God.

> JESUS CAME TO BRING AN UPSIDE-DOWN KINGDOM, A KINGDOM THAT'S COUNTERINTUITIVE AND SURPRISING IN THE BEST OF WAYS.

Without Jesus' work of bringing the new covenant, His command to take up our crosses, die to ourselves, and follow Him would be impossible. But that's the beauty of being a follower of Christ. Sure, there are a lot of hard things Jesus asked of His disciples and of us today, things that go against our natural instincts. Yet, praise be to God, dear friend. Praise be to the One who has not left us alone to stumble our way around in the dark, aimlessly shuffling around, running into foreign objects, and stubbing our toes.

"I am the light of the world. Whoever follows me will not walk in darkness but will have the light of life" (John 8:12).

"Come to me, all who labor and are heavy laden, and I will give you rest," He said. "Take my yoke upon you, and learn from me, for I am gentle and lowly in heart, and you will find rest for your souls. For my yoke is easy, and my burden is light" (Matthew 11:28–30).

Taking up Jesus' yoke, walking with Him side by side in this thing called life, requires one thing: commitment. The *ESV Study Bible* says it requires "making a commitment."[13] Oftentimes it feels like committing to the Lord and following what He says—especially when it comes to releasing our desire for control—are anything but simple. But here's the catch. When we stop resisting His commandments for our lives and actually get to know His heart, we realize that what He asks is not burdensome. When we surrender our stories, we realize that's exactly what we were created for. Not because God wants robots who just nod their heads and say yes without any personality or life flowing through their veins, but because God has abundant life for His children—and the only way it's found and truly enjoyed is through surrender, trust, and faith.

Warning: Work in Progress

I've thought many times that my life should come with a warning label for my people in real life and online to see. Not because I'm some sort of tornado-like klutz but because it is so painfully clear to me that I am still a work in progress.

Throughout this book, I've shared a lot about my story with chronic illness and my death grip on control. Honestly, I have shared more than I ever thought I would. It has felt scary and healing all at the same time, admitting my weaknesses, struggles, hidden sins, and deficiencies. It has been amazing to testify of God's goodness, faithfulness, and provision in the past. So I feel like it's only fair to bring you up to speed on where my story is today—right here and now.

As I write this chapter, I recently celebrated my twenty-third birthday. This has been an interesting birthday to celebrate because it seems very "in between." It's not quite as exciting as a sweet sixteen, twenty-first, or even thirtieth birthday, in my opinion. But as each birthday tends to encourage us to do, I have found myself looking back on where I've been, looking at where I am now, and looking forward to where I'm going.

In my personal reflection I've realized one thing.

My life does not look like I thought it would in a lot of ways.

Instead of going to college, graduating with a biology degree, and getting into medical school, I am writing this book and spend most of my days teaching women about Jesus, online and off. Instead of having ample energy and a clean bill of health, I am a chronic illness warrior of nearly nine years. Instead of marrying my high school sweetheart right away in my "perfect" timeline, I ended up waiting almost five years. Instead of holding off to have kids until we were a few years into marriage, my husband and I are weeks away from meeting our first baby. Surprise to us but not a surprise to God.

If you were to ask me what I thought about all of those things a few years ago, I likely would have cried. I likely would have described the way my life had turned out in terms of derailments, pitfalls, and wrenches thrown into my perfectly calibrated plan.

But where I saw derailments, failed plans, and broken dreams, God saw the bigger picture. He had it all under control. He saw my fists clenched down hard on what I thought I could control, but He never cast me out. He never made fun of me for thinking I was in the driver's seat with full control of the wheel. Instead, He continued to love me, patiently wait on me, and remind me (sometimes not so gently) that I was not in control, and that's okay.

One of the most obvious ways God continues to teach me to surrender is through my struggle with fibromyalgia. You remember how it all began: in bed, unable to move due to gut-wrenching pain, and deeply depressed. Now almost nine years later, I praise God for the way He has brought me through. No, God has not taken this cup away from me. He has not healed my body or sent me into remission. Day in and day out, I wake up with my fibro-friend, but it is worlds different from how it was when I was fourteen.

Instead of spending days upon days in bed with excruciating pain, I can usually get out of bed in the morning. I am able to manage the pain and get through most days with enough energy to work, take care of the house, serve my husband, and love on other people. I have taken full advantage of modern medicine, naps, setting boundaries, and moving my body. All have been gifts from God to help me heal during this chronic illness journey. All have been stepping stones that helped me go from paralyzed in bed to living life each day—able to work well, serve well, and very soon, take care of our baby boy well.

I've had countless conversations with loved ones and received numerous DMs on Instagram asking if I ever wished that I had never been diagnosed with fibromyalgia. This question usually makes me chuckle, because it seems as if it should be a question with a "Duh, of course" kind of answer. But as cheesy as it sounds, I don't think I would change a thing. If genies and three magic wishes were real, I don't think I would use one of my wishes to alter time and live in a world where I was never diagnosed with fibromyalgia.

Sure, the hospital visits sucked. The physical therapy felt impossible. The pain has made me weep, keel over, and scream at God more times than I can count. The ways in which I was limited, isolated, and cut off from the world plummeted me into a dark place at times.

But God, being the amazing Redeemer that He is, used all that pain and all the things I thought were U-turns in my story to teach me this invaluable lesson of surrender. He used and continues to use all of it to remind me I'm not in control.

I've learned that independence is overrated, and dependence on Him is where we really find strength.

I've learned that when I yield myself to Him, I can trust Him with my story.

I've learned that patience isn't a poison—it's a gift to weather life's storms and disappointments.

I've learned that God has given me everything I need to live this abundant life for Him. He is not hiding, and I do not need to have it figured out—and thankfully, I don't have to do any of this alone. The Holy Spirit is my power source.

I've learned that the more I know who God is through time spent in His Word, the more I will love Him and the more I will be able to surrender my story.

And I've learned that unless I build my life upon His truth and His Word, my foundation will crumble, and I will clench my fists once again and crawl back to the myth of control.

You see, sweet friend, that's the difference between our stories in Christ and the stories the world gives us. The world preaches a self-help gospel with its chief goal to brainwash people into believing they can manifest, control, and summon the life they desire from good vibes and personal achievements. The world will tell us we don't need anyone and if we don't have our five-year, ten-year, or even fifteen-year plans in place, then we're doing something wrong.

But it is for freedom that Christ has set us free (Galatians 5:1). The world may preach an attractive message that appeals to our old self before we were saved, but it will only lead to slavery. It will only lead to illusions of control (it's just that: an illusion, not reality), and then when things inevitably don't go our way, we're left disappointed, frustrated, and angry. It's a vicious cycle.

But I'll never stop saying it. There is good news in Christ. He offers a way to break that cycle. It's a three-step process we must repeat every single day.

1. Take up our crosses.
2. Die to ourselves.
3. Follow Him.

Your Story of Surrender

I am so thankful for the ways in which you've let me share my story throughout these pages. I want you to know how truly seen, loved, and cherished you are by God. (And I'm sure if we could get to know each other in real life, I'd be a pretty big fan of yours too!) Yet I don't want us to close this book and put it back on the shelf without talking about your life—your beautiful, precious life.

I've shared what the surrendered life has looked like for me, through my struggles with chronic illness, unfulfilled longings, and trust issues. But you have your own story to surrender. We may share similar feelings or moments, but you have been purposefully given a handcrafted story from the Creator of the universe.

Know this: your life does not have to look like mine or anyone else's to be surrendered to God. Your circumstances and individual personality will not look exactly like mine. That's because the surrendered life is not one-size-fits-all. Granted, I'm not saying we can form our own definitions of surrender, because we know it's the same command for all believers—taking up our crosses, denying ourselves, and following Jesus—but it's lived out in our own unique lives in different ways.

For example . . .

The surrendered life looks like my in-laws, releasing their control and their ideas of what they thought life would look like after walking away from their steady jobs and the security that came with them, and instead trusting God to direct them on a new path.

The surrendered life looks like my husband and me, completely shocked by our surprise pregnancy just four months into our marriage, but completely trusting God to provide. We are so excited, and God is so good to us. Even if it was not a part of our plan, it was a part of God's all along.

The surrendered life looks like the single woman wondering if she will ever find the love of her life and get married. Instead of letting disappointment and bitterness creep in, she is determined to keep running her race for the Lord and make the most of every season He has placed her in.

The surrendered life looks like the young man who has absolutely no clue what to do with his life—what college to attend, what job to pursue—but instead of worrying, he follows God in faith, even if it seems as if he's stepping forward blindly.

The surrendered life looks like the woman who has operated out of self-sufficiency and independence her whole life but has found herself utterly exhausted and in need of change. Instead, she admits her need for God's sovereignty and control over her life and no longer sees these things as weakness but as strength.

The surrendered life looks like the couple who is struggling with infertility and realize that God uses the waiting not as a punishment but as an opportunity to exercise patience and to trust God more.

The surrendered life looks like being completely okay with not knowing all the answers or having the five-year plan figured out, because God is in control and we know that His plans are for our good, our sanctification, and His glory.

At the end of the day, the surrendered life acknowledges that it's all about Jesus. The surrendered individual knows that "for from [God] and through him and to him are all things" (Romans 11:36). The surrendered individual knows God is their ultimate helper—that this may be the hardest thing they ever learn to do, but God is the only One who can help them do it.

But What If I Don't Feel Like It?

One of the biggest hurdles I have come across when it comes to surrender is the lack of *desire* to do so. We know in our hearts that surrender is better than control. Deep down inside, we really do know the truth. But when it comes to actually *wanting* to release control and let someone else have the reins of our lives, it feels absolutely backward. It feels helpless, vulnerable, powerless, and scary. It's like someone telling us to let go of the steering wheel of our car and trust that it will not crash as we fly down the freeway at seventy miles per hour. No one in their right mind would do that easily or willingly, right?

It must come down to cultivating a desire to follow God and say yes when He tells us to surrender. But how do we do that? How do we go from surrendering just out of duty to surrendering because we want to? How do we genuinely desire to surrender to God and trust Him when it goes against everything inside us? When we'd rather have control over our lives because it is more comfortable? When it feels less scary to trust ourselves than open up our lives to whatever unknown God may throw at us?

Psalm 37:4 says, "Delight yourself in the LORD, and He will give you the desires of your heart." This is a verse I often see taken out of context, but I understand why. It seems pretty straightforward at first glance, right? It sounds as if King David is saying just to be happy in God, and if you're happy, not negative, He will give you whatever you want. But as we learned in the last chapter, we need to look at God's Word as it was intended. Time to put on our biblical sleuthing hats once again.

What David was trying to drive home in this verse is that when God's children take delight, or find their true satisfaction in God, their hearts will desire the right things—the things that are aligned with God's own desires and will for them. I love how Scottish biblical scholar and Baptist minister Alexander Maclaren explained it: "Longings fixed on Him fulfill themselves."[14]

That, my friend, is the key to desiring the right things. Practically, you and I can live Psalm 37:4 by praying each day, asking God to help us take delight in Him and find our satisfaction in Him alone. Not in the world, our jobs, our financial situations, our relationship statuses, or even how our five-year plan is shaping up. Becoming satisfied and content in God can be achieved by spending regular time in the Word—soaking up His promises, letting His truth transform our hearts, convict our spirits, and teach us about His character. The more we know God and what He has to say, the more our new hearts, these hearts born out of Jesus' gift of salvation, will find satisfaction in Him.

On the days when we just don't feel like surrendering to

God, we can pray through our feelings: *God, You know my heart. You know my thoughts and feelings before I even express them. You know that I am struggling right now to desire the things of You. You know that I am fighting against my old flesh. Please help me to desire what You desire. Work through my stubborn heart and help me to be disciplined enough to prioritize the truth of Your Word over my own changeable feelings. I really do want to know You, find my satisfaction in You alone, and surrender my story.*

I find great hope in knowing that God is in it for the long haul. God is the God of the long game. Unlike you and me—who can only catch dim glimpses of the next day, not to mention the next few years—God has a bird's-eye view. In His wisdom and sovereignty, He sees it all. That's why we can trust Him when He promises to do sanctifying work in us. Sanctification is God's system, God's process of setting His people apart, of transforming us to be holy just as He is holy.

So when you're tempted to settle into despair or frustration, remember that He who promised is faithful. Remember that God's work of sanctification in our lives takes time. If we've given our lives to Christ, we can rest assured knowing that He is working on us daily. We can rest assured knowing that a part of God's plan of sanctification for our lives is helping us become better surrenderers and better trusters. He asks that we reciprocate by giving our love, our effort, and our discipline—sticking with Him and following Him as He refines us.

Remember, it's a unique and beautiful gift to be able to give God the glory in our surrender. And, as a matter of fact, it's not just our story. It's *His* story. Ephesians 2:10 reminds us: "For we are his workmanship, created in Christ Jesus for good works, which God prepared beforehand, that we should walk in them."

Paul also wrote, "I have been crucified with Christ. It is no longer I who live, but Christ who lives in me. And the life I now live in the flesh I live by faith in the Son of God, who loved me and gave himself for me" (Galatians 2:20).

IT'S NOT JUST OUR STORY. IT'S *HIS* STORY.

Like my good friend, Karen, once told me, "We're written into God's story—not the other way around."

We were created by God and for God, not for ourselves. Isn't it time that we switch our thinking? When we realize that the life we've been given through Jesus' sacrifice on the cross is not of our own effort, a supernatural shift occurs. We can't help but surrender our stories because they are really His anyway. As Paul said in Galatians 2, it is *Christ* who lives inside of us and directs and empowers all we do. The stories we live are now being generated by our faith in Jesus. Moment by moment, we have the ability and the beautiful gift to trust God's work in our lives.

When we keep our eyes fixed on the Creator instead of the circumstance . . . when we choose to trust God's Word over our feelings . . . when we release our death grip and lift up our lives with open hands to God, we will never be disappointed by the way our stories play out. We don't have to be afraid of what may come of our lives.

It's time we set down our pens and let God write His story in the most beautiful, divine ink. Taste and see that He is good and trustworthy. Believe that because He created you, He knows what is best for you. Trust me: He is a far better storyteller, writer, and fulfiller than we could ever hope to be!

Take a deep breath with me.

Ready, set, surrender.

A Prayer of Surrender

Steal this prayer, or create a version of your own to pray on your journey toward the surrendered life.

Lord, help me surrender my story to You each and every day, remembering that I can only do so through Your Spirit and strength.

When I'm tempted to rush ahead of Your timeline, remind me to wait upon You.

When the world feeds me the lie that I can do all things in my own strength, bring me to my knees.

When my soul is anxious, reassure me that there is no safer place to be than in great need of You.

When I am trying to figure it all out, remind my heart to pray, "Not my will but Yours be done."

Thank You for revealing what I need to know to make decisions that honor You. Thank You for revealing Your beautiful heart and trustworthy character to me—I know I can trust You with my story.

Thank You for the gift of the Holy Spirit, my counselor, guide, power source, and advocate.

Lord, I trust Your will. I trust Your heart. I will keep declaring these truths back to You, training my heart to trust You even when it's not easy.

I love You, Lord. Thank You for loving me so much that You want to write my story. Amen.

Acknowledgments

Michael, my sweet husband. Thank you for believing in this message and my words even before all of this came to be. More than that, thank you for believing in our Great Author and leading not only myself but now our sweet little boy in His way. You are the definition of a prayer warrior—one who bears my burdens and always encourages me to live out of rest and reverence for our Lord. Your steadiness and strength have emboldened me to keep running my race for the Lord. I am so thankful I don't have to run alone, because you are right there beside me. Thank you also for the little things (that are really big things) like holding our sweet babe when I needed to meet editing deadlines, ordering takeout when I'm too exhausted to cook, and making me laugh on the daily. We have had many exciting conversations about how God is going to use this book, and I'm grateful for you, my hype man. It is my greatest honor and privilege to be yours. I love you.

Hunter, my sweet boy. Someday, when you're old enough to read, I pray that this message would touch your heart, because after all it's really God's message. I pray that the girly cover won't scare you away from diving deep into these pages. You, my sweet boy, are my joy, my delight, and my gift. You are evidence that God gives the best gifts in His timing—the best timing. You are proof that God is worthy to be trusted. Every day I pray that you would come to know, love, and live for the God who authors your story. I feel ridiculously blessed to be your mama and a part of your story. God is already writing a beautiful one for you, and I can't wait to see how it continues to unfold with each day. I love you with all that I am.

Dad and Mom, my built-in best friends. Thank you for your faithful love, support, and encouragement all these years. I know there is no such thing as perfect parents, but you two come close in my eyes. I am so grateful for the countless conversations we have had over dinner or on the couch about this message. In many ways you both helped form this book. Dad, thank you for demonstrating what it means to be a godly leader. Thank you for raising Lee and me in a house that always keeps God at the center of our lives and the conversation. You are my hero. Mom, thank you for serving me and our family so selflessly. You inspire me to lay down my life at Jesus' feet every day. You are the definition of service, and I want to be just like you when I grow up. I love you both endlessly.

Lee, the best big brother. I hope you know that your fiery yet steady faith inspires, challenges, and encourages me. You set the standard for what it means to love people without restraint, serve people without exception, and boldly trust God with your story. Not everyone can say that their brother is one of their closest and best friends, but I am thankful that I can. You're the best. End of story.

Wes, Shawna, Matthew, and Mark, the greatest in-laws a

girl could ask for. While I fell in love with Michael, I also fell pretty hard for you guys. Thank you for welcoming me into your family many summers ago and never looking back. You are collectively and individually some of the sweetest gifts in my life from our Father above. Thank you, Wes and Shawna, for relentlessly praying over me and this book. I can't tell you how much I treasure our relationship and respect the heck out of your legacy of faith. Thank you, Matthew and Mark, for always bringing the laughs and the joy of the Lord to my life. I love you all deeply.

Teresa, the best literary agent a girl could ask for. You are affectionately known as my "book mom" to everyone in my life and I couldn't think of a more accurate description. When I say I couldn't have gotten through this process without you, I mean it with every fiber of my being. Thank you for being my advocate, my mentor, and my cheerleader. I prayed for an agent that not only was incredible at their job but one whose heart also felt burdened for this message of surrender. And God led me to you, the answer to that prayer. You have not only taught me so much about publishing but about the Lord and His Word, and for that I'm forever grateful. You're the real deal. I love and admire you so much.

And to Bill Jensen, the fiercely gifted leader of the William K. Jensen Agency. Thank you for your expertise and support. I can't thank you enough for going to bat for me and welcoming me into the WKJ family.

Daniel, my editor. You, my friend, are deeply gifted at what you do. I am endlessly thankful for how you not only have walked me through this process and refined this message but also how you have spiritually counseled me in many ways. Thank you for taking my countless calls, emails, and texts over the last year.

This work is not for the faint of heart, but you have brought so much joy and fulfillment to it. Thank you, thank you.

To the entire Thomas Nelson / HarperCollins Christian team. Thank you for taking a chance on a small-town girl from Oregon. Thank you for believing in this message, not because I'm "all that," but because God is. I prayed that the publisher I chose would share a heart for biblical literacy and a fierce devotion to God's Word and people. Thank you for being that for me and this book. We're only getting started.

My sweet friends and family, every one of you. You are a blessing, pure and simple. Not a day goes by that I don't thank the Lord for your friendship and the way you influence me for the better. Thank you for being ever so faithful and constant. I'm blown away that I get to be even a small part of your story. Thank you for being a big part of mine. Love you big!

Notes

1. Thomas Troward, *The Edinburgh and Dore Lectures on Mental Science* (New York: Cosimo, 1909; repr., Radford, VA: Wilder, 2008), 52.
2. William McKane, *Proverbs: A New Approach* (London: Student Christian Movement Press, 1970), 495.
3. Jon Bloom, "The Insanity of Leaning on Our Own Understanding," Desiring God, March 7, 2014, www.desiringgod .org/articles/the-insanity-of-leaning-on-our-own-understanding.
4. Bloom, "Insanity of Leaning on Our Own Understanding."
5. Ben Stuart, "Kings and Kingdoms: When God Shoots Down Your Plans," November 15, 2021, in *Passion City Church DC*, podcast, MP3 audio, 35:22, https://passion-city-church-dc -podcast.simplecast.com/episodes/kings-kingdoms-when-god -shoots-down-your-plans.
6. This three-part outline for the life of Joseph appears in many sermons and published works. For example, see David Jeremiah, "God of the Pit, the Prison, and the Palace," CBN News, August 1, 2019, https://www1.cbn.com/cbnnews/cwn/2019/august/david -jeremiah-god-of-the-pit-the-prison-and-the-palace.
7. Peter Scholtes, "They'll Know We Are Christians," copyright 1966, F.E.L. Publications, assigned to The Lorenz Corp., 1991.
8. *Merriam-Webster.com Dictionary*, s.v. "omnipotent," accessed

October 21, 2022, https://www.merriam-webster.com/dictionary/omnipotent.

9. *Merriam-Webster.com Dictionary*, s.v. "omniscient," accessed October 21, 2022, https://www.merriam-webster.com/dictionary/omniscient.

10. Chandler Moore, Jonathan Edward Jay, Nathan Walter Jess, Tony Brown, "Man of Your Word," copyright 2020 © Bethel Music Publishing, Capitol Christian Music Group, Capitol CMG Publishing, Integrity Music, Kobalt Music Publishing Ltd.

11. R. C. Sproul, *The Promises of God: Discovering the One Who Keeps His Word* (Colorado Springs: David C. Cook, 2013), 8.

12. Roy B. Zuck, *Basic Bible Interpretation: A Practical Guide to Discovering Biblical Truth* (Colorado Springs: David C. Cook, 2002).

13. *ESV Study Bible* (Wheaton, IL: Crossway, 2001, ESV Text Edition, 2011), 1972.

14. A. Maclaren, *The Expositor's Bible: The Psalms* (1892), released by Project Gutenberg, March 31, 2013, https://www.gutenberg.org/files/42445/42445-h/42445-h.htm.

About the Author

Through the *Truth Talks with Tara* podcast, her Instagram community, and other resources, Tara Sun passionately teaches women of all ages how to know, love, and live God's Word for themselves. She shows how to break down God's Word into understandable pieces, while also adding an artistic flare through her digital art. Tara is married to her high school sweetheart, Michael, and is a mom to their newest addition, Hunter. You'll find them living and serving the Lord in Oregon.